Prestel Museum Guide

The Frances Lehman
Loeb Art Center
Vassar College
POUGHKEEPSIE, NEW YORK

The History and the Collection

D1087067

PRESTEL
Munich · Berlin · London · New York

Imprint

Financial support for this publication has come
from the Friends of the Frances Lehman Loeb Art Center

© Frances Lehman Loeb Art Center and Prestel Verlag,
Munich · Berlin · London · New York 2007
© for the images by Frances Lehman Loeb Art Center,
Vassar College, Chip Porter
© for artists' rights see page 144

Front cover Marsden Hartley, *Indian Composition*, 1914, see page 99
Back cover Frances Lehman Loeb Art Center, see pages 12–13

Prestel Verlag
Königinstrasse 9, 80539 Munich
Tel. +49 (0)89 38 17 09-0; Fax +49 (0)89 38 17 09-35
www.prestel.de

Prestel Publishing Ltd.
4, Bloomsbury Place, London WC1A 2QA
Tel. +44 (0)20 7323-5004; Fax +44 (0)20 7636-8004

Prestel Publishing
900 Broadway, Suite 603, New York, NY 10003
Tel. +1 (212) 995-2720; Fax +1 (212) 995-2733
www.prestel.com

Library of Congress Control Number: 2007920614

British Library Cataloguing-in-Publication Data:
a catalogue record for this book is available from the British Library;
Deutsche Nationalbibliothek holds a record of this publication
in the Deutsche Nationalbibliografie; detailed bibliographical data
can be found under: http://dnb.ddb.de

Project Management Julia Höffner
Text Editing Chris Murray, Chester
Design and layout a.visus, Michael Hempel, Munich
Origination ReproLine mediateam, Munich
Printing and binding Passavia, Passau

Printed in Germany on acid-free paper.

ISBN 978-3-7913-3836-1

Contents

The History of the
Art Museum at Vassar College 4

The Collection 16

Information 142

The History of the Art Museum at Vassar College

Previous pages
Early plaster casts of classical sculpture
in the galleries, late nineteenth century.

The history of publicly collecting art in the United States, compared to that of European nations, seems hardly a history at all. The major public museums were by-products of the tremendous untaxed wealth enjoyed by American captains of industry during the fourth quarter of the nineteenth century. The Museum of Fine Arts in Boston and the Metropolitan Museum in New York were founded in 1870. The Philadelphia Museum of Art was founded in 1876 (although its sister institution in Philadelphia, the Pennsylvania Academy of Fine Arts, stemmed from Charles Willson Peale's early nineteenth-century cabinet of curiosities), and the Art Institute of Chicago in 1879. What such proud cities, burgeoning with cash, undertook in America's 'Gilded Age' was already in place at colleges and universities in the northeastern United States. The Yale University Art Gallery dates back to 1832, making it the oldest art museum in the United States, while the Bowdoin College Art Museum's collections date back to 1811, though its museum opened its doors in the 1890s. Dartmouth College claims natural history collections dating back to the 1770s. Yet, the original Vassar College Art Gallery, the precursor to the Frances Lehman Loeb Art Center, was founded as an original part of the college in 1864, making it the first college or university to open with an art museum as an integral part of the academic program.

Matthew Vassar, a transplanted Englishman, brewer and businessman, was convinced that his college should have an active component of instruction in the visual arts. A gallery was part of architect's James Renwick's plan for the college from the outset in 1861. The question before the trustees was what to put in the gallery. Here, opinions differed at first. In 1863, trustee Charles Raymond recommended the hiring of a "first class artist" to produce paintings while instructing students by example as they watched him paint. This way the gallery would be filled after ten or fifteen years and the students served. Presumably, this plan was not attractive to Vassar for he was already in negotiations in that year, via the college's first president, Milo P. Jewett, with Emma Church, an American artist living in Italy, to provide copies of the great works of Italian art for the gallery. Two paintings were paid for by the trustees, but when Church requested the staggering sum of $1,200 to copy the Madonna del Foligno by Raphael, the trustees rebelled and Vassar ended the relationship by absolving the college of any further commitment to this plan, and agreed to buy the painting personally, although the trustees later absorbed the costs, which had by then escalated to $1,500. All the Emma Church copies now reside in the permanent collection. Further,

Henry Van Ingen, the first professor of art at Vassar,
with a student ca. 1889–1898.

during 1862/63, a trustee committee on the Art Gallery was preparing its
own set of recommendations. Members of this committee included the
painter and inventor Samuel F. B. Morse, the historian Benson Lossing, and,
most important of all, the Baptist clergyman and avid art collector and
theorist, Elias Lyman Magoon. Magoon was the chairman of the committee
on the Art Gallery and the voice behind its report, which was presented
formally to the full board in 1864. He had already put together a large collection of small canvases by Hudson River School and National Academy of
Design artists, as well as a large number of drawings, watercolors, and prints
documenting the historical topography of Great Britain and parts of contin-
ental Europe. He was violently opposed to a gallery consisting of copies and
was able to convince Vassar of his judgment and connoisseurship in the
matter of choosing art, so much so that when Magoon threatened to resign
as a trustee over the Church copies, Vassar did everything he could to ap-
pease him, including making a special trip to Magoon at his home in Albany
to pacify him, late in 1863. At that point, Vassar saw for the first time the art
collection that Magoon had been assembling for the past twenty years and

Vassar's study collection in the late nineteenth century.

was greatly impressed with its quality. From this moment, Vassar placed all his trust in Magoon on artistic matters and was convinced that the college should purchase his collection to get the gallery off on the right foot.

The report of the trustee committee on the Art Gallery was issued in February 1864, and is a triumph of inflated, late Victorian rhetoric of a kind that gives us a window onto Magoon's ardent personality and considerable powers of persuasion. The language of the twenty-page report is so much *sui generis* that it resists all efforts to summarize it. Hence several lengthy quotations may serve to capture its essence:

Art is diviner than science; the latter discovers, this creates. It is the highest sagacity and purest exertion of human nature. The study of it possesses this great and peculiar charm — that it is absolutely detached from the disgraceful contests of sordid ambition. Above and beyond all petty strifes, mankind are most attracted and united by a taste for beautiful art — a taste at once the most engrossing and ennobling, refining the imagination and fortifying the judgment, elevating emotion to the loftiest enthusiasm, and, at the same time, perfecting the critical faculty, under the joint influence of subjugated sense and sovereign reason …

Take the gem of your prospective college, under the full sway of legitimate education. Draped in enraptured unconsciousness, her bosom swells, cheeks flush, eyes sparkle, and thrilling inspiration gleams on her brow, as all that is receptive and immortal within responds to the living words of a competent teacher expounding facts in the presence of things … You may double your expenditure in monumental structures, or in lifeless apparatus, and yet not attain an iota of educating force. That is not a medicinal bath — something soaked in — but latent ability educated forth. When all other tools of inert erudition are at hand, give them to a substratum of LL.D.'s, with a substratum of D.D.'s and all you will thereby accomplish is the dignified extinguishment of what little capacity for excellence yet remains in American youth, as you might smother a swarm of young bees under a cart-load of autumnal leaves.

On the contrary, lay your material foundation deep and broad; cumulate languages, sciences, and art, in as huge an aggregate as possible; but, in God's name, send to the center — fire! From at least one chair let positive electricity neutralize the prostrating influences of all the rest. For that purpose, collect an ample and diversified gallery of actualities in artistic elegance — forms, tints, tone, true to every kingdom of nature, and which shall at once illustrate the loftiest principles and refine the most delighted hearts.

Magoon and the committee then went on to address specifically what the collection should comprise. In order of priority they singled out "at least one hundred oil paintings by as many different masters as possible … at least sixty must be first-rate transcriptions of American landscape mainly along the Hudson, Lake George, New Hampshire, and Vermont." Then, they called for at least a hundred watercolors recording the "great monuments of Rome, Venice, Florence, Genoa, Paris, and London," including historical ruins of castles, abbeys, and battlefields. After that, they cite such objects as armor, antiquities, coins and, finally, prints. If this proposed collection for Vassar sounded strongly for the most part like a description of Magoon's own collection, it was scarcely a coincidence for, by the time the report was delivered, Magoon had decided to sell his collection to Vassar for $20,000 (or roughly $250,000 today). The transfer of the collection was made by the summer of 1864 and in August of that year Vassar wrote to Magoon and expressed the maudlin yet accurate sentiment that he was humbled when he considered "how many eyes will hereafter be gazing upon these Gems while the Collector, and donor bones lies mouldering in the grave."

Thus, the Magoon collection established the points from which the art collection at Vassar would grow. The appointment of Henry Van Ingen, the first professor of painting and curator of the gallery in 1865, would insure the stewardship of the collection. While the collection did not grow greatly in size during the period of Van Ingen's tenure through 1898, a number of key works were acquired, including Hubert Robert's Octavian Gate and Fish Market (1784, p. 59), the stunning set of seven large watercolors by William Trost Richards on thematic aspects of England (1882, p. 93), and the popular American painting Shadow Decoration by Charles Courtney Curran (1887, and the first purchase of the new gallery, p. 94).

Collection growth remained desultory until the gallery moved into a new arts building, Taylor Hall, completed in 1915. A large collection of over sixty American reproductive engravings was given in 1916, and the great leap forward for the collection took place in 1917, when college trustee Charles M. Pratt (also donor of the building) gave sixteen Italian Old Master paintings (purchased with the advice of noted Finnish art historian and connoisseur Osvald Sirén), including works by Bachiacca (p. 40) and the two large Ulysses panels now attributed to the Master of the Johnson Collection Assumption of the Magdalene (p. 30). Pratt also added a large collection of Chinese jades to his gift, part of which was later deaccessioned and sold in the 1980s. The acquisition of such a group of early Italian panel paintings was key to the collection's development and made it a place where students could use original art of high quality in the aid of their historical studies without necessitating a trip to an urban center such as New York City, Boston, or Hartford. The period around the First World War also witnessed the arrival of the successor to Van Ingen's post as professor of painting. Clarence Chatterton, an 'American Scene' painter and close friend of Edward Hopper, arrived at Vassar in 1915 and stayed until 1948. During his long tenure, he not only influenced the course of many students' lives, but his own art found its way into the Poughkeepsie community and some of it returned to the Vassar collections. Chatterton was part of an excellent art department that counted among its members the august if somewhat punctilious department chairman and late Victorian temperament, Oliver Tonks; Arthur McComb, a young Harvard-trained Italian art specialist who helped the study of Italian Baroque painting regain validity in America; the young instructor A. Hyatt Mayor, who was destined to become a legendary curator of prints at the Metropolitan Museum of Art; and the socially well-connected

The Vassar College Art Gallery ca.1960.

firebrand, Agnes Rindge, who came to Vassar in 1923. In many respects, it was Agnes Rindge who had the biggest impact on the art collections for the next thirty years.

Rindge, who also pursued her graduate studies at Harvard, made friends there with a group of bright young men who, like her, were students in Paul Sachs's famous museum course. These included Alfred Barr (later the first director of the Museum of Modern Art), Kirk Askew (later director of Durlacher Brothers, the influential New York art gallery), Arthur Everett ('Chick') Austin (innovative museum director of the Wadsworth Athenaeum), and academic Henry Russell Hitchcock. Both Barr and Hitchcock would later, at different moments, teach at Vassar. They and other Harvard friends such as Edward M. M. Warburg would not only pursue serious study in historical phases of art but would also be champions of contemporary art and cultural life and bring Rindge into contact directly or indirectly with a range of modern artists, choreographers, composers, and photographers,

The Frances Lehman Loeb Art Center,
designed by Cesar Pelli, which opened in 1993.

from Alexander Calder to Lincoln Kirstein to Virgil Thompson to George Platt Lynes. While the decade of the 1920s did not result in major gifts to the collection, the seeds that were planted in the classroom among students ready to embrace all that was modern would later bear fruit as those instincts, cultivated in youth, would result in active lives as art collectors and, later, as benefactors to their *alma mater*. Rindge herself, in the course of her life, would give or bequeath to Vassar over fifty works of art, the first in 1932 and the last, at her death, in 1977, including the great early mobile of Calder, The Circle, of 1934 (p. 114).

College and university collections tend to grow in sporadic surges forward. For Vassar, the next such surge would arrive in 1941, when it received several sculptures and 170 Old Master engravings, etchings, and woodcuts on the seventieth anniversary of the birth of banker and collector Felix M. Warburg

of New York City, thanks to the influence of Warburg's granddaughter Carol Rothschild, who had recently graduated from Vassar. Warburg, who died in 1937, had amassed a superb print collection under the tutelage of William Ivins, the curator of prints at the Metropolitan Museum. His collection was particularly strong in the sixteenth-century German masters from Schongauer to Dürer, Baldung and the so-called *Kleinmeister*, as well as the work of Rembrandt. The bulk of this collection was bequeathed to the Met, but as a number of them were already in their collection, the Warburg examples were not needed. This was particularly true of Dürer's works, since the Met had just recently acquired the complete Dürer collection of Junius P. Morgan, so even the best of the Warburg Dürers were viewed as redundant. This generous decision benefited the Vassar collection greatly and resulted in many of the finest examples of the graphic arts finding their way to the College's collection (pp. 32, 34, 36). Also donated by the Warburg family were fine examples of late medieval and Renaissance northern European sculpture including the elegant Late Gothic chalk Madonna and Child Holding an Apple (p. 24). Another key ingredient in the Warburg family's decision was the recent arrival on the Vassar faculty of the German émigré scholar Richard Krautheimer, who taught at Vassar from 1935 to 1952 and was a formative influence on Miss Rothschild. His reputation and charm had greatly impressed the Warburgs, so much so that they offered him the post of director of the then as yet unrealized Jewish Museum.

Following the Warburg gift, the next key event in the evolution of the collection was not to center on the Old Masters but rather on American Moderns. The New York based music critic Paul Rosenfeld (1890–1946) was a frequent contributor to the little magazine *The Dial* during the 1920s. There, he wrote often of progressive composers such as Stravinsky, Schoenberg, Bloch, and Copeland among others. He also wrote for *The Nation, The New Republic,* and *Vanity Fair.* In addition, he was a frequent visitor to Alfred Stieglitz's gallery (and the subject of one of Stieglitz's finest portraits) and there purchased work by Arthur Dove, Georgia O'Keeffe, Marsden Hartley (p. 98), and John Marin. Edna Bryner Schwab, a Vassar graduate and fellow habitué of Stieglitz's gallery, became the executrix of Rosenfeld's estate following his death in 1946. This led to the gift of fifteen Stieglitz-circle modernist works to the collection in 1950 from Rosenfeld's estate. This important clutch of modernist paintings and works on paper was followed by Schwab's own bequest in 1967 of fifty-two more works, featuring major paintings by Georgia O'Keeffe (pp. 101, 102, 103), watercolors by Marin, and even photographs by Stieglitz and Edward Weston. These two collections alone made Vassar a point of interest for those wishing to study the rise of modern art in America.

Other important donors of modern art to the collection included Blanchette Hooker Rockefeller (class of 1931), who over the course of five decades added works of considerable importance to the collection, including the key paintings by Francis Bacon (p. 131), Karel Appel (p. 126), Ben Nicholson (p. 132), and Mark Rothko (p. 118). A second source of complementary postwar European and American art was donated during the 1990s from the collection of Katherine Sanford Deutsch (class of 1940), bringing to the Vassar students and faculty the opportunity to study from major original works by Joan Miró (p. 124), Willem de Kooning (p. 123), Balthus (p. 122), Jackson Pollock (p. 120), and Arshile Gorky (p. 117), to name but a few. In recent years, the photography collection has experienced a resurgence, and new areas of collecting have been opened up such as Japanese and Outsider art. The original gift of Matthew Vassar to his college has grown now to over seventeen thousand works of art from all time periods and geographical points of origin, thus contributing to the efficacy of the liberal arts education at Vassar. It is presently housed in a modern building, designed by architect Cesar Pelli, which opened in 1993, thereby expanding our ability to bring work of the finest quality to our students, faculty, and regional public.

James Mundy
The Anne Hendricks Bass Director

Head of the Viceroy Merymose

Red granite, H. 27 3/4 inches (70.5 cm),
Egyptian, Dynasty 18, Period of Amenhotep III, ca. 1375 BCE.
Gift of Margaret Lanphier Wengren, class of 1938.

This is the effigy from the outer sarcophagus of Merymose, the Viceroy of Kush (Nubia) under Amenhotep III. The head was removed with other fragments from the exterior sarcophagus at his tomb in Thebes' Gournet-Mourrai by robbers in the nineteenth century, well before its official excavation and 'discovery' in 1937. This sculpture is the most important antiquity in Vassar's collection. The hairstyle and beard demonstrate that the deceased has become divine through his assimilation by the god Osiris. On top of his cranium is written in hieroglyphics the message: "The words are spoken — I have surrounded my brother in Osiris, Merymose, whose limbs shall not be weary." There are portions of Merymose's granodiorite intermediate and interior sarcophagi in the Museum of Fine Arts, Boston, and the British Museum, London.

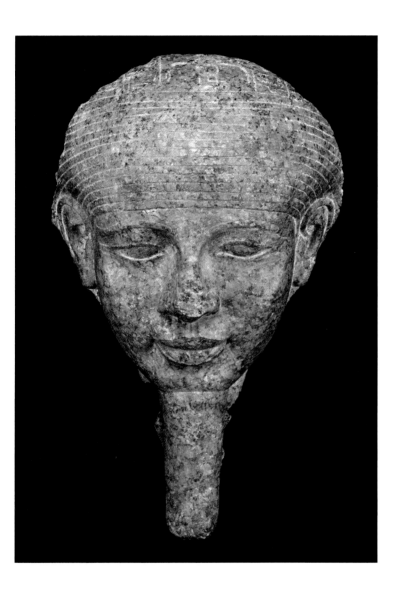

Cista

Bronze, 10¹/₄ × 8 inches (26 × 20.3 cm),
Etruscan, third century BCE.
Transfer from the Vassar College Classics department in 1968.

This bronze container from the ancient city of Praeneste in Etruria (present day Palestrina) is one of over a hundred similar objects discovered in excavations near the site of the once famous temple dedicated to Fortuna. Conventional wisdom holds that they were used exclusively as cosmetic cases for wealthy women, though there is increasing support for the view that they were also used as funerary urns since some have been found to contain ashes. The distinctly masculine iconography of the Vassar cista includes wrestling figures on the handle who could be Peleus and Atalanta grappling at the funeral games of Pelias; figures leading horses labeled "Castor" and "Pollux" (in the archaic spelling "[P]ORLOU[CES]"), and other figures including Silenus with his wineskin, Jupiter (identified as "Dies Pater"), Juno, and Diana. The winged figure leading the procession could be Lasa (or Nemesis), the Etruscan deity of Destiny. The unusual combination of characters and the mistakes in labeling suggest an amalgamation of several narrative prototypes. The cista came to Vassar when it was purchased from the sale of the William Randolph Hearst Collection in 1941. The graceful incised drawing suggests the model from which both Cocteau and Picasso found inspiration for their highly linear styles in the 1930s and 1940s.

Denarius
Silver, 1 inch in diameter (2.5 cm),
Roman, 47/46 BCE.
Transfer from the Vassar College Classics department.

This silver denarius was issued by Julius Caesar during the civil war as part of the African campaign against Cato the Younger that ended in the battle of Thapsus. It shows on the obverse (heads) a bust of the goddess Venus facing right and wearing a diadem; on the reverse (tails) stands Aeneas holding the *palladium*, a wooden statue of Pallas taken from Troy, in his right hand, and carrying his father Anchises over his left shoulder. The story of Aeneas' travels from Troy to Italy and Latium, recounted by Virgil in the *Aeneid*, was a central myth of the Romans, but the type is personal to Julius Caesar as well: Venus was his patron goddess, for whom he built the temple of Venus Genetrix, and Aeneas was his ancestor. The type of 'traveling Aeneas' was also appropriate to the African context of the coin since Aeneas' abandonment of Queen Dido of Carthage and her subsequent suicide explained the historical enmity between Rome and the city in North Africa and predicted that Rome, and Caesar, would be victorious in the current struggle as well. The use of the public coinage, and public myth, for what we would call personal propaganda is emblematic of the downfall of the Roman Republic at the hands of ambitious politicians and generals like Caesar.

Tower

Earthenware with green glaze, H. 34¹/₂ inches (87.6 cm),
Chinese, Eastern Han Dynasty, second century CE.
Gift of the Schloss Collection.

Towers such as these formed part of the tomb goods of affluent landholders. They reflect the contemporary conditions in the Chinese countryside during troubled times, when landholders were forced to defend their holdings with private armies and fortifications. This particular tower, excavated like so many others throughout central China possibly in the province of Shaanxi, is not decorated with soldiers and bowmen, as many others are, but with what seem to be nobles or officials seated on the parapets and in front of the entry. Its dignity suggests a purpose more ceremonial than defensive. The highly decorated architecture of the tower with its apricot leaf acroteria on the roof, together with the latticework and crossmark incisions, call attention to the special rank and significance of the building. Asian art was not a collecting interest at Vassar until the second decade of the twentieth century, and the curriculum has grown significantly in this area during the past thirty years. This has encouraged the growth of the art collection outside the traditional focus on the Western intellectual tradition.

Front Panel from a Child's Sarcophagus

Marble, 17^1/$_2$ × 58^1/$_2$ inches (44.5 × 148.6 cm),
Roman, third century CE. Gift of the Friends of the
Vassar College Art Gallery and Noma and William Copley, by exchange.

This sarcophagus panel, decorated with a chariot race among erotes, com-
memorated the passing of a young girl. In translation, the inscription reads:
"Dominus Flavius Chrysion the father, and the mother of the daughter
Cossutia Flavia, the sweet one of five years." The marble was probably
imported from Asia Minor and the inscription possibly added at a later date.
The idea of a chariot race among winged children is fantastic, but the details
of the race are quite accurately rendered, down to the tower-like building,
behind the third eros from the left, decorated with the sculpted eggs used to
count the laps around a typical hippodrome. The race itself is conveyed with
the action and confusion of horses and riders in pitched competition, some
of the characters portrayed in triumph, others crashing in defeat. While the
custom of holding chariot races as part of funerary games has a long history
in ancient Greek and Roman history and literature, going back to the *Iliad*
of Homer in the eighth century BCE, one may also read in this contest a
symbolic meaning. The race represents the passage of time, with the specter
of an early death being implied in the defeat of at least one of its child-like
contestants.

Madonna and Child Holding an Apple

Chalk with traces of paint, 26^1/$_4$ × 9^1/$_8$ × 6^1/$_2$ (66.7 × 23.2 × 15.9 cm),
French, ca. 1400. Gift of Mrs. Felix M. Warburg and her children.

Part of a very important gift to Vassar of a large portion of the collection of New York financier Felix M. Warburg, this splendid example of Late Gothic French chalk carving was thought, until 1945, to be a plaster cast, but then laboratory analysis determined it is an original carved sculpture in chalk of the 'schöne Madonna' type. Its workmanship is precise and the folds of the draperies fall in the gentle, rhythmic cascades distinctive of Late Gothic high style. Residual traces of orange pigment on the faces, of red and blue on the Madonna's garments, and of gilding on her crown point to the certainty that the sculpture was once a brilliant example of French polychrome sculpture. The manner of the figures is courtly, yet the Child is portrayed as playful and beaming. Scholars are of the consensus that the work is the product of a Parisian workshop, and that the stone was quarried in the region around Rouen.

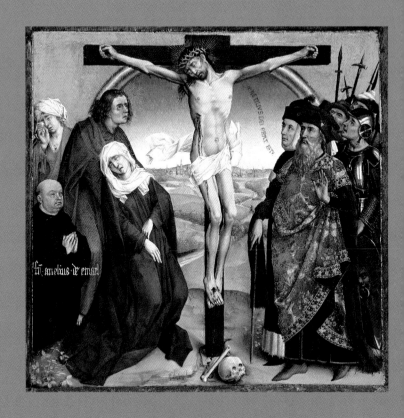

Crucifixion with the Donor Brother Aurelius of Emael

Oil on oak panel, 14 × 14¹/₄ inches (35.6 × 35.8 cm), ca. 1465.
Museum Purchase, Betsy Mudge Wilson, class of 1956, Memorial Fund;
Charles M. Pratt Fund; Suzette Morton Davidson, class of 1934, Fund;
Francis Woolsey and Helen Silkman Bronson, class of 1924, Fund.

Up until the acquisition of this fine example in 1995, Vassar owned no
northern European painting of the fifteenth century. The present example,
deaccessioned from the collection of the New York Historical Society, where
it had resided since 1867, is an immaculate example of the physical realism
of Early Netherlandish painters in the tradition of Jan van Eyck, and of the
emotional realism that issued from the studio of Flanders' other great practitioner, Rogier van der Weyden of Brussels, in whose studio the artist of this
panel trained. The precise rendering of the green and golden brocade of the
judge's robes and the lancet windows reflected in the armor of the soldier
testify to the ability of this anonymous artist. Issuing from the mouth of the
judge are the Latin words: *re filius dei erat iste* (truly the Man was the Son of
God). Technical analysis has determined that the artist made several
changes to the composition, including adding the donor figure, prominently
identified as "Fr[ate] Aurelius de Emael," after the panel was completed,
necessitating the repositioning of the hands of the grief-stricken Virgin
from a gesture similar to that of the donor's praying gesture to one of
collapse. Before being given to the New York Historical Society, the painting
was owned by Thomas Jefferson Bryan (1802–1870), a New Yorker who
amassed a large collection of Old Master paintings between 1830 and 1850,
later installed in the Bryan Gallery of Christian Art on Lower Broadway in
New York City.

Lazarus and the Rich Man

Tempera, ink, and gold on vellum, 6 3/8 × 7 1/2 inches (16.2 × 19 cm),
French, ca. 1515–1520. Bequest of Sarah Hamlin Stern,
class of 1938, in memory of her husband, Henry Root Stern, Jr.

This page from a complete book of hours likely originated from the manuscript workshops of Tours. The book contains over ninety full, half, or quarter page illuminations following the usual cycles for such books. These begin with the sequence of calendar months, each illustrated with the appropriate labor and list of the feast days. Then there follow the prayers for the eight canonical hours — Matins, Lauds, Prime, Terce, Sext, None, Vespers, and Compline — each illustrated with a full-page illumination. Also included are prayers for other occasions, including the Mass for the dead. The illustration that conjoins the psalm to be said at Vespers in the evening is that depicting the rich miser, Dives. The story, from Luke 16, recounts how the rich man spurned the beggar Lazarus when he came to him asking for crumbs from his table. When they both died, the rich man was tormented in Hell by seeing Lazarus borne to Heaven by Abraham. The illustration complements the text of the psalm, which speaks of earthly sorrows and tribulations. Contrasting this message is the visual gaiety of the marginal decorations that include elegant renderings of dragonflies, snails, peacocks and numerous recognizable blooms such as iris, pansy, dogwood, and violet.

Ludger tom Ring the Younger (attributed to)
The Open Missal

Oil on oak panel transferred to masonite, 26¼ × 26¼ inches (66.7 × 66.7 cm),
German, mid-sixteenth century. Museum Purchase, Mrs. John D. Rockefeller 3rd
(Blanchette Hooker, class of 1931) Fund.

This strikingly realistic *trompe l'oeil* representation of a late medieval illuminated manuscript is one of a small number of similar objects produced in Germany in the sixteenth century. An identical painting is in the collection of the Uffizi in Florence. The painting is meant to fool the eye by showing the manuscript as if a sudden breeze had begun to turn the pages of the open book. All the surfaces of the book have been rendered with exactitude, including the vellum pages, the leather straps, and their metal buckles. The ruffled pages have obscured most of the full-page miniature of the Crucifixion on the right, complete with its golden border decorated with lilies of the valley, columbine, corn flowers and other blossoms and insects. The purpose of such a painting is not fully understood; however, it was most likely set up on a lectern in order to surprise a visitor. The attribution to Ludger tom Ring the Younger is based on similar works given to the artist, and to the presence of the words "Ludevi rinki" under the first line of musical notes, practically the only legible words of text in the entire composition.

The Master of the Johnson Collection Assumption of the Magdalene

The Adventures of Ulysses:

The Blinding of Polyphemus (top)

The Battle with the Laestrygonians (bottom)

Both tempera on panel, 31¹/₂ × 63¹/₂ inches (80 × 161.3 cm),
early sixteenth century. Gift of Charles M. Pratt.

These two large rectangular panels are part of a series of which at least one more panel, depicting The Return of Ulysses, is known. Because of their elongated rectangular shape and their mythological subject, these panels have long been thought to be front sections of Italian *cassoni* or storage chests, yet this theory seems unlikely given that they are really much too large for this portion of a typical *cassone*, and furthermore that none of the panels shows the keyhole carved in most *cassone* of this kind. The stories depicted on the panels are continuous narratives portraying several scenes from Homer's epic tale. The first shows Ulysses and his comrades gouging out the giant's single eye and then, to the right, Ulysses' men fooling the Cyclops into allowing them to pass by covering themselves with sheep skins. Further to the right, Polyphemus discovers that he has been deceived and hurls a giant boulder at the departing ships. To the left, the goddess Athena in the sky wreaks devastation on the walled city of Troy. Below to the left, Ajax Oileus is blasted by an angry Poseidon. The stories of the second panel begin with Ulysses kneeling before King Aeolus, the keeper of the winds, who provides the crew with good sailing winds and bags of storm winds to keep below decks. When a jealous crewmember accidentally opens one of the bags, the resulting storm blows them off course and onto the island inhabited by the Laestrygonians, who kill several members of the crew and then drive Ulysses' men back to sea with a barrage of stones. To the far right, in the middle ground, Ulysses' men arrive on the island ruled by the enchantress Circe, who turns one of them into a wild boar.

There has been much study and many opinions given as to the identity of the author of these unusual panels. The consensus regarding the authorship and the date is that it is the work of an as yet unknown painter who trained with the Florentine artist Lorenzo di Credi around 1500. Based on other works by the same hand, he is known by the painting of the Assumption of the Magdalene in the Johnson Collection at the Philadelphia Museum of Art.

Albrecht Dürer (German 1471–1528)

Adam and Eve

Engraving on tan paper, 9$^{13}/_{16}$ × 7$^9/_{16}$ inches (24.9 × 19.2 cm),
1504. Gift of Mrs. Felix M. Warburg and her children.

This large engraving by Dürer is a technical *tour de force* and, at the time of its execution, Dürer's *summa* on the subject of printmaking, extending his powers of illusion in this art form far beyond that of any practitioner to date. The delicate hatching that forms the shading of the abdomen of Adam, for example, is composed of small organized universes of lines completely under the control of a master. The figure's proportions and pose are derived from the sculpture of classical antiquity, an early appearance of this influence in the art of Germany. In this print, the Garden of Eden is transformed into a northern European forest inhabited by a number of animals at rest, in addition to the First Parents succumbing to the temptation of the serpent. These animals have been interpreted as symbolizing each of the four classical humors or fluids that, according to medicine of the time, dictated the personalities of individuals when out of balance. Adam and Eve was one of over one hundred and fifty works of art donated by the family of Felix M. Warburg to Vassar in 1941 following the great banker and philanthropist's death. The Vassar gifts were dominated by prints by Dürer and Rembrandt, and form the core of a very strong Old Master print collection.

Albrecht Dürer (German 1471–1528)

Saint Jerome in his Study

Engraving on tan paper, 9³/₄ × 7¹/₂ inches (24.8 × 19 cm),
1514. Gift of Mrs. Felix M. Warburg and her children.

Dürer devoted the years 1513/14 largely to the art of engraving. During these years he produced three large engravings of both visual and iconographic complexity—The Knight, Death and the Devil; Melencolia I; and Saint Jerome in his Study—collectively known as the *Meisterstiche* (masterpieces of engraving). In his image of Saint Jerome, Dürer surpasses even his Adam and Eve in terms of the subtlety of the use of his engraver's tools to suggest not only the soft light filtering into the saint's scholarly chamber, but also the textures of the wood grains on the interior and the soft fur of the sleeping lion and dog in the foreground. The perspectival organization of the scene is very strictly laid out according to scientific principles well known to Dürer and illustrated in the treatise on drawing that he produced late in his life. The sophistication of the dappled patterns of light playing across the surfaces of the room is far beyond that of any artist's printmaking achievements of the day. It is no wonder that Dürer gave this print to his hosts and the dignitaries he met during his travels.

Albrecht Dürer (German 1471–1528)
The Virgin Crowned by Two Angels
Engraving on tan paper, 5⁷/₈ × 4 inches (14.9 × 10.2 cm),
1518. Gift of Mrs. Felix M. Warburg and her children.

While this engraving is not as imposing in its size as those by Dürer listed above, it is noteworthy in the Vassar collection because of the quality of its printing and its condition. The German Dürer scholar Josef Meder assigned alphabetical categories to all of Dürer's prints based on the freshness of the impression. Thus, a Meder 'A' rating would suggest a print made from the newly engraved plate. The 'B,' 'C' or an even lower category would suggest subsequent printings, often after the plate had been reworked or, even, a print taken after the artist's death. The Virgin Crowned by Two Angels is a glorious example of a Meder 'A' engraving, pristine and sharp in its line and rich in its inking, so that the full effect of the folds and shadows of the drapery or the sticks of the wattle fence are maximized. For print collectors, condition is everything, and Felix Warburg's collection clearly identified him as a connoisseur of great distinction.

Lucas van Leyden (Dutch ca.1494–1533)

Susanna and the Elders

Engraving on tan paper, 7⅝ × 5⅝ inches (19.4 × 14.3 cm),
ca. 1508. Gift of Mrs. Felix M. Warburg and her children.

The reputation of the Dutch painter and engraver Lucas van Leyden has been
overshadowed by that of his German contemporary, Dürer. He was, however,
capable of innovative presentations of narrative, as is the case here. Traditional portrayals of Susanna, the Old Testament heroine, spied on while
bathing, normally place her in the foreground and include the elders in the
middle or background peering from their cover. Lucas, however, reverses this
orientation and places us in the elders' space, thereby focusing our attention
on the interaction of two voyeurs as they regard the rather chastely dressed
Susannah dangling her legs in the stream in the background. She is in-
cidental to the main story, the foolishness of the two men, idly gawking and
displaying openly such morally questionable behavior. This engraving dates
from around 1508, when Lucas first started making prints. His later works
are clearly dated on the plates.

Circle of Joos van Cleve
Saint Jerome in his Study
Tempera and oil on panel, 38³/₄ × 32³/₄ inches (98.4 × 83.2 cm), ca. 1530.
Museum Purchase, Friends of the Vassar College Art Gallery Fund.

This painting is one of at least six replicas of a lost prototype by Joos van Cleve, based in turn on the painting of the same subject by Albrecht Dürer now in Lisbon. Other Flemish artists also produced variants on this composition, raising the total number of extant similar images to at least a dozen. The version closest to that at Vassar resides in the collection of the Harvard University Museums. Vassar's painting was deaccessioned by the Art Institute of Chicago in 1985, where it was part of the Harding Collection. The painting is intended as a *memento mori* (reminder of death) portraying the saint in a pensive 'brown study,' pointing to a skull. The message is reinforced by the piece of paper reading *respice finem* (consider your end) adhered to the wall over the niche that holds the kettle and basin. In other variants of this painting, the message reads *homo bulla* (man is a bubble) or *cogita mori* (think of death), all expressing the same message of preparing spiritually for the end of earthly things. Jerome, who translated the Bible into Latin, was considered by Renaissance artists an early Humanist scholar, hence he is often portrayed among the books, quills, ink, and the other trappings of learning. The inscription on the book before him on the lectern reads simply "text." Among those on the shelf above the saint are the Book of Revelations inscribed "Apocalipsis," and presumably a volume of the Epistles of Paul, only the first four letters of "Epistolas" being legible. Paul was a favorite author of Jerome and one with whom he felt an historical and philosophical attachment. Other iconographical elements attest to the saint's affinity with the purity of the Virgin, including the metal ewer, the basin, and the white towel. The corked carafe on the shelf holding a liquid seemingly composed of rose petals in suspension was also used as a visual metaphor for Mary's virginity in late medieval art. The vase next to the Crucifix on the shelf contains, among other flowers, the columbine, a symbol of the Sorrows of the Virgin.

Francesco d'Ubertino Verdi, called Il Bachiacca (Italian 1494–1557)

The Baptism of Christ

Oil on panel transferred to canvas, 39 × 31³/₄ inches (99.1 × 80.6 cm),
ca. 1523. Gift of Charles M. Pratt.

The artist known as Bachiacca was, according to Vasari, like Raphael a Florentine student of Perugino and a friend of Andrea del Sarto. He was part of a generation of painters in Florence during the mid-sixteenth century who did not follow the more flamboyant Mannerist model of painting exemplified by the work of Pontormo and Rosso Fiorentino, but rather continued a conservative presentation modeled after Perugino and Ghirlandaio. The Vassar Baptism of Christ is a theme that he portrayed on several occasions. The present painting is really a condensation of figural motifs found in a larger version of the subject now in Berlin. This adaptability allowed him to satisfy the needs of patrons on many different levels of commissions.

Oil on panel, 16³/₄ × 22¹⁵/₁₆ inches (42.5 × 58.3 cm), ca. 1600.
Gift of Marjorie W. Sherburne Prescott.

Pieter Brueghel the Younger, the eldest son of the great Flemish painter of peasant genre scenes of the same name, and the brother of Jan Brueghel, the floral painter, followed very directly the successful model of his father and provided many copies and variants of his father's themes to the Flemish art market. In the case of Spring, it is one of four depictions of the seasons of the year made as a set of engravings by Pieter van der Hayden after drawings by Pieter the Elder. The prints were published by the workshop of Hieronymous Cock in 1570. It is possible that the elder Brueghel also executed a set of paintings on this theme that was recorded in a mid-eighteenth-century inventory of the Viennese *Schatzkammer* (treasury). It is clear that the younger Brueghel made quite a cottage industry from copying the designs of his father, for there are at least ten surviving versions of this painting alone. The painting portrays the seasonal outdoor labors of springtime in the manner of calendar illuminations from medieval books of hours. A group of male and female peasants cultivate a geometric arrangement of raised flowerbeds already featuring the early blooming tulips, while two fine ladies visit the garden. Behind them, two laborers prune a fruit tree while others shear sheep in the middle ground below. In the background beyond the garden, peasants dance outdoors and a field is used to bleach linen in the sun. Such a painting, probably executed in the early seventeenth century, testifies to a later generation's interest in benign and nostalgic genre painting of a bygone era.

Francesco Barbieri, called Il Guercino (Italian 1591–1666)

The Presentation in the Temple

Pen and brown ink with brown wash on tan paper,
10⁷/₁₆ × 15³/₁₆ inches (26.5 × 38.9 cm), 1626/27. Museum purchase.

This superb drawing by the prolific Bolognese Baroque artist known as Guercino (the 'Squinter') is a preliminary study for one of the frescoed lunettes in the cupola of the cathedral at Piacenza. The entire project was executed between May of 1626 and November of 1627. Guercino's best drawings demonstrate the lively and sure-handed feeling found in this one. In this drawing, the exceptional flourishes of the pen line and the quick and confident application of the wash create a monumental feeling. The drawing once belonged to Dan Fellows Platt, an important collector of Guercino's drawings and a major donor to Princeton University. Vassar College was at the forefront of art museums that collected Baroque art in the 1930s and 1940s. Much of this interest arose from faculty members such as Agnes Rindge, whose friendships included that of A. Everett 'Chick' Austin, director of the Wadsworth Athenaeum in Hartford, an early evangelical voice for Baroque art. The drawing itself was bought for Vassar by Richard Krautheimer, who was then professor of art, in 1941.

Christoffel Jegher (Flemish 1596–1652/53)

Susanna and the Elders

Woodcut, 17^1/$_2$ × 22^{13}/$_{16}$ inches (44.5 × 57.9 cm), ca. 1635.
Museum purchase, Francis Woolsey and Helen Silkman Bronson,
class of 1924, Fund.

This woodcut demonstrates a collaboration between the skillful printmaker
Jegher and the pre-eminent painter of the seventeenth century in northern
Europe, Peter Paul Rubens. Their collaboration arose through Rubens's work
with the Plantin Press in Antwerp, where Jegher was employed as a woodcut designer for the press's books. The subject of Susanna spied on by the
two elders comes from the apocryphal Book of Daniel. When she refuses
their advances, they slander her. It was a theme used in art throughout
the sixteenth and seventeenth centuries as a moral cautionary tale about
the evil of bearing false witness. However, in painting, it also provided an
opportunity to present a blatantly sexual theme featuring a lovely female
nude to an audience who become as involved in the voyeurism as the elders
themselves. This print is one of nine woodcuts made by Jegher after
Rubens's designs and carries an inscription that states that Rubens obtained
a 'privilege' for this design, an early form of copyright meant to discourage
copyists.

Andrea Vaccaro (Italian 1604–1670)
Erminia and the Shepherds

Oil on canvas, 69¹/₄ × 91³/₈ inches (175.9 × 232.1 cm), ca. 1650.
Gift of Charles M. Pratt.

Traditionally attributed to the Neapolitan Baroque artist Mattia Preti, this large painting was reassigned to the work of Andrea Vaccaro in the 1980s. It portrays the sixth and seventh stanzas of Canto VII of Torquato Tasso's (1544–1595) epic poem *Gerusalemme Liberata* of 1575, a source of inspiration for many artists and composers of the Baroque era. Erminia was the daughter of the Saracen King of Antioch. Her love for the Christian knight Tancred (in spite of his own love for Clorinda, a female warrior) takes her to the Christian camp dressed in armor like Clorinda to look for the wounded Tancred. Discovered and pursued by the Christian guards, she escapes to the countryside, where she happens upon "a white haired man in the cool shade, weaving twig baskets, with his flock nearby and listening to three children's lullaby." The unexpected soldier startles the group, but she reassures them by taking off her helmet "showing her eyes and her fair golden locks." While the moment is a minor one in the narrative poem, it is a splendid opportunity for the artist to present the dramatic confrontation of the elements of war and peace, reconciled with a single gesture.

Pieter Claesz (Dutch 1597/98–1660)
Banquet Still-Life with Ewer and Bread
Oil on panel, 27⁷/₈ × 39 inches (70.8 × 99 cm), 1641.
Gift of Mrs. Lloyd Williams in memory of her father, Daniel Cotter.

Pieter Claesz was one of the foremost still-life painters in the Netherlands during the seventeenth century. He worked in Haarlem for his entire career. He is primarily known for his 'breakfast' or 'banquet' still-lifes, of which this is an excellent example. Often these works would include, in their well-composed materials, references to the concept of *vanitas* — items related to the fleeting pursuit of the material things of this world at the expense of the more lasting spiritual values. The Vassar painting presents a rich table decorated with, among other things, elegant, shiny pewter and silver plate, and glass roemers, as well as a luxurious figural salt cellar, an early pocket timepiece with its case, and a long-necked ewer on which closer inspection reveals the convex reflection of the artist seated, painting at his easel. The composition builds impressively in scale from right to left on a diagonal beginning with the void of the crisp white linen tablecloth in the lower right and ending with the long glass flute on the left. The further diagonal play of the parallel ovals of the platters and small bread loaves creates cohesion, as if those on the perimeter revolve around the central platter with its roasted fowl like the planets around the sun. Indeed, the roemers act almost like moons in a kind of orbit. In addition, the tendrils of the grape vine emerging from the bowl of fruit continues the sinuous arabesque visual play of the ewer's handle and dragon neck. A 'hidden' symbolism might also be understood in the presence of the cruciform timepiece, a reference to the transitory nature of worldly things as well as a Christian reference to the cross. Also, the bread and grapes are probably references to the Eucharistic body and blood of Christ's sacrifice.

Salomon de Braij (Dutch 1597–1664)

Odysseus and Circe

Oil on canvas, 42^1/$_2$ × 36 inches (108 × 91.4 cm), ca. 1650.
Museum Purchase, Pratt Fund; Francis Woolsey and Helen Silkman Bronson,
class of 1924, Fund; Betsy Mudge Wilson, class of 1956, Memorial Fund;
Suzette Morton Davidson, class of 1934, Fund.

Salomon de Braij was born in Amsterdam but had moved to Haarlem by the time he was twenty years old. There he was a student of Hendrick Goltzius and Cornelis van Haarlem. De Braij had a varied career in Haarlem, not only painting portraits and small histories, but also designing silver work and architectural projects. Documents also refer to him as a poet. His portrayal of Odysseus and Circe, the moment when Odysseus seeks to rescue his companions turned into swine by the sorceress, is presented with a high degree of classical *decorum*, yet also a feeling for common details of behavior, as in the way the hero slouches at the table while holding his wine glass, unable, according to Homer, to eat or drink owing to sadness over the fate of his companions. While the servant pours a long stream of wine into a goblet, the gesture of temperance according to contemporary emblem books, Circe advances, her wand hidden in the folds of her drapery. Her spells will prove ineffective on Odysseus owing to an herb he was given by Hermes to neutralize Circe's powers. While the painting takes place in a classical palace decorated with sculpture including a figure of Apollo, the father of Circe, the figures themselves suggest the plain features of the contemporary Dutch middle-class rather than the exotic or heroic appearance of mythical characters. The presence of the pigs, wine cooler, and the servants gives the scene an everyday quality. Thus, the painting is to some extent history and to an equal extent a genre presentation.

Rembrandt van Rijn (Dutch 1606–1669)

The Death of the Virgin

Etching and drypoint on tan paper, 15⅝ × 12⅝ inches (39.7 × 32.1 cm), 1639.
Gift of Mrs. Felix M. Warburg and her children.

This etching is one of Rembrandt's largest, grandest, and most theatrical. Unusually for the largely Protestant Netherlands, this image seems to have been meant for a Catholic audience, among whom the cult of Mary was still alive and such narrative moments as this one, drawn from apocryphal legends, were popular. While it owes a debt to similar prints by Dürer, Rembrandt invests the work with a grandiloquence that matches some of his works as a painter at a time when he was intent on demonstrating his superior talents on the grandest scale possible, whether in history painting, portraiture, or printmaking. As if to enhance the theatrical impact of the scene, Rembrandt separates the viewer from the action by creating more of a stage setting in the foreground, a distance that also allows us to appreciate the heavenly and supernatural display that occupies almost one-half of the space. This device, almost paradoxically, creates a landscape out of an interior view.

Rembrandt van Rijn (Dutch 1606–1669)

The Three Trees

Etching with burin, drypoint and sulfur tint on tan paper, 8³/₈ × 11¹/₆ inches
(21.3 × 28.1 cm), 1643. Gift of Mrs. Felix M. Warburg and her children.

This image was Rembrandt's most technically ambitious landscape. It was
produced by reworking a plate that originally bore another grand-scale
etching, his Death of the Virgin of 1639 (see preceding). Traces of the angels
above the bed of the dying Virgin in that etching were transformed by
Rembrandt into clouds in this one. Originally thought to reproduce an actual
location, this print is now considered an imaginary composition by the artist,
highly refined in its organization. The seeming meteorological battle of calm
and storm taking place in the windswept Dutch landscape dominated by
the three trees (themselves a possible suggestion of the three crosses of
Golgotha) challenge Rembrandt's powers of graphic evocation and demonstrate his skills at the top of their range. Writers on this print are fond of
pointing out the pair of lovers hiding almost unnoticed in the bushes in the
lower right-hand corner of the composition, some imputing symbolic significance to their activity. According to Edward M. Warburg, this etching was
one of his father's favorite prints and was displayed prominently in the print
room of the Warburg mansion on Fifth Avenue in New York City (now the
home of the Jewish Museum).

Daniel Vosmaer (Dutch 1622–1669/70)
View of a Dutch Town with a Ruined Wall
Oil on wood panel, 26 × 20⁷/₈ inches (66 × 53 cm),
ca. 1662. Purchase, Agnes Rindge Claflin Fund.

Daniel Vosmaer was a native of Delft and painted in that city for almost
his entire career. According to documents, he moved from Delft to the town
of Den Briel in 1665/66. Vosmaer survived the horrific 'Delft Thunderclap'
of 12 October 1654, when eighty to ninety thousand pounds of gunpowder
exploded in an underground depot, leveling or damaging hundreds of
houses and killing scores of residents. The aftermath of the explosion provided local artists, including Vosmaer, with an unexpected subject matter.
Vosmaer painted both portrayals of the explosion itself and more lyrical
scenes of the activities of daily life restored to the partly ruined town. While
there are no specific landmarks to support the supposition, it certainly
appears as if the artist took this broken wall and its adjoining house as a creative visual element against which to situate the once more verdant town
parklands. His use of the wall as both barrier and introduction to the scene
is a clever compositional device and also a poetic reference to time, transformation, and the folly of man's enterprises on earth.

Salvator Rosa (Italian 1615–1673)
Landscape with Herdsmen
Oil on canvas, 29¹/₂ × 39¹/₂ inches (74.9 × 100.3 cm), ca. 1661.
Gift of Mrs. William Levitt (Janice Loeb, class of 1935).

Salvator Rosa was trained as an artist in Naples and by 1635 was working in
Rome. Between 1640 and 1649 he was painting in Florence. In addition to
being a painter, he received recognition for his printmaking, poetry, and act-
ing. While he painted his share of religious subject matter, he made his
greatest contribution as a landscape artist, often including a subsidiary
story within an evocative or emotionally charged landscape. Such subjects
could be taken from ancient history or mythology, literary sources such as
the writings of Tasso, or images of bandits and brigands on the land. His
landscapes were not classically beautiful like those of Claude Lorrain or
Gaspard Dughet, but rather rugged and occasionally stormy, often setting a
psychological tone for the moment depicted. Rosa was also drawn to darker
subjects of a violent nature, including unusual portrayals of witches' Sab-
baths and battles. This painting is fairly typical of his more romantic landscapes, placing a pair of herdsmen and their animals in a carefully con-
structed, diagonally organized landscape where the curving forms of the
trees and rocky cliff almost take on the appearance of a wave breaking on the
shore. Devices such as these and the blasted tree trunks were the elements
that impressed nineteenth-century American landscape painters such as
Thomas Cole and encouraged their assimilation of the Baroque tradition in
the depiction of a largely fictive natural world.

Luca Giordano (Italian 1632–1705)
Saint Dorothy of Cappodocia
Oil on canvas, 40 × 29¹/₂ inches (101.6 × 73.7 cm), before 1692(?).
Purchase, Friends of Taylor Hall Art Gallery Fund.

Giordano's Saint Dorothy, probably painted in the 1690s, was acquired by Vassar in 1937 (for the price of $250), thus representing an early acquisition of an Italian Baroque painting by an American art museum. Baroque painting was unpopular among public institutions during the first third of the twentieth century, American collectors preferring the more traditional accepted taste found in Italian Renaissance works. This orientation would change drastically in the 1930s thanks to omnivorous American collectors such as John Ringling and Walter Chrysler, and influential art museum tastemakers such as A. Everett Austin at the Wadsworth Athenaeum in Hartford, Connecticut. The director of the Vassar Art Gallery in the 1930s was Professor Agnes Rindge, a friend of Austin's and a member of a social circle that included many who championed modern art, and who also appreciated Baroque painting for its energy and its flouting of Renaissance painting's conventions. This work by Giordano, whose nickname was Fa Presto (literally 'make haste'), has the dynamism that is a hallmark of this Neapolitan painter and includes the rich colors that derived from his appreciation, late in his career, of the work of Venetian artists such as Paolo Veronese. It is signed clearly on the stone ledge by the artist and is likely a work that originates from the years just preceding his departure from Florence to Madrid in 1692. A possible pendant for this painting with the same dimensions, depicting a half-length image of Saint Catherine, has recently been discovered in a Neapolitan private collection.

Giovanni Battista Tiepolo (Italian 1696–1770)

Time Seated Clutching a Putto

Brown ink and wash over traces of graphite on tan paper, 8⁷/₈ × 11⁹/₁₆ inches (22.5 × 29.4 cm), ca. 1750. Museum purchase.

Primarily described in a mixture of thick and thin brown washes, this drawing is one of a series of studies made by Tiepolo in preparation for his frescoed ceiling in the Palazzo Clerici, Milan. It entered the collection in 1934, making it another Baroque acquisition made early in the period when American museums were taking an interest in the Baroque. Tiepolo was a master of economy in his drawings, being able to suggest a state of mind or an emotion with a brisk coating of wash. For example, on this sheet, the washes used to create the putto's eyes and mouth suggest, with just a few blots of ink, that it is crying. Time's somewhat demonic smile is also suggested in this manner. The drawing is one of a number in the same style featuring Time as the subject. Others are in the Metropolitan Museum and the Pierpont Morgan Library and Museum, New York.

Trompe L'oeil Still-Life of a Letter Rack

Oil on canvas, 32 × 46¹/4 inches (81.3 × 118.5 cm),
Italian, eighteenth century. Gift of Henrietta Roig,
mother of Josephine Roig Humphrey, class of 1945.

This is one of a group of paintings of card racks and smal objects set against pine cupboards designed to fool the eye by their verisimilitude. They were produced in Italy at the end of the seventeenth and beginning of the eighteenth centuries by a number a little known artists working in a very similar fashion in cities in central and northern Italy. Among the artists linked to the Vassar painting are Antonio Gianlisi the Younger (Veneto 1677–1727); Christoforo Munari (Reggio Emilia 1667–1720); Domenico Remps (Venice late seventeenth century); Antonio Cioci (Florence ca. 1732–1792); Jacopo Palmieri (Turin 1737–1809). The connections derive from the use of the same medals, prints, drawings, and reliefs, as well as other elements, in two or more of the paintings. For example, the small relief plaque of the putti and the goat on the left of the Vassar painting also appears in one by Cioci, as do other elements such as the eyeglasses hanging on the rack, and the red and black chalk drawing of a head of a woman. The prints by Stefano della Bella also turn up in drawings by Palmieri. The keys, timepieces, similarly addressed letters and the staple of *trompe l'oeil* — the simulated housefly resting on the plaster medallion portraying Glaucus and Scylla — occur in many of these works. In the Vassar painting, there are a number of references to Florence and the Medici, including the appearance of the prints by Stefano della Bella and Jacques Callot, who both worked for the Medici, as well as the plaster medallion in the lower left depicting Francesco de' Medici (1614–1634), who died of disease at the age of twenty fighting in the Thirty Years' War. The other medallions portray, in the lower right, Louis XIV of France (1638–1715), the grandson of Marie de' Medici, and, in the upper right, Cosimo III de' Medici (1642–1723).

Felice Boscaratti (Italian 1721–1807)

Atlas Maintaining the Balance of the World
(or The Moral Asylum)

Oil on canvas, 48³/₄ × 38¹/₂ inches (123.8 × 97.8 cm), before 1772.
Gift of Mr. and Mrs. R. Kirk Askew.

Folly Changing the Course of the Universe
(or Life and the Economy of the Universe)

Oil on canvas, 49¹/₂ × 38 inches (125.7 × 96.5 cm), before 1772.
Purchase, Friends of Taylor Hall Art Gallery Fund.

These two paintings comprise half of a commission given to the Veronese painter Felice Boscaratti by a local doctor, Lazzaro Riviera. Their subject matter consists of an allegorical system of almost incomprehensible subtlety drawn up by the commissioner as a series of philosophical lessons for young men. They were so difficult to understand that Riviera had copies engraved after the four original paintings and inscribed with Latin texts. He also published a pamphlet, *La Educazione Virile*, in 1773 in an effort to explain the paintings. The paintings were taken to Venice when Boscaratti moved there and they were there when he became the official painter of Giorgio Pisani, who was elected Procurator in 1780. Upon his election, the paintings were hung along a processional route, but their abstruse symbolism was interpreted by the local Inquisitors as subversive. Fearing sedition, they arrested Pisani four days later, and his artist was directly affected by the disgrace of his patron, at whose trial he was required to testify. While the overall content of the paintings remains obscure, we are able still to understand, in the first painting, the warning contained in the figure of Mars, who treads on a learned tome, unbalancing the equilibrium of the world, while in the other painting, Pan plays his bassoon-like instrument and dances, as wild animals rend apart another expensive volume of learning. Thus, martial and sensual pursuits are the enemies of scholarship, and the arts are victimized by the excesses of passion when it triumphs over reason. These scenes are painted as simulated unstretched canvasses, introduced to the viewer in the Atlas allegory by a contemporary gentleman, who affixes an inscribed sheet of paper to the canvas, and in the Pan allegory by a pair of ancient philosophers or scholars. In the second *trompe l'oeil* canvas, the curling, unpainted and exposed edge carries an inscription mentioning Lazzaro Riviera.

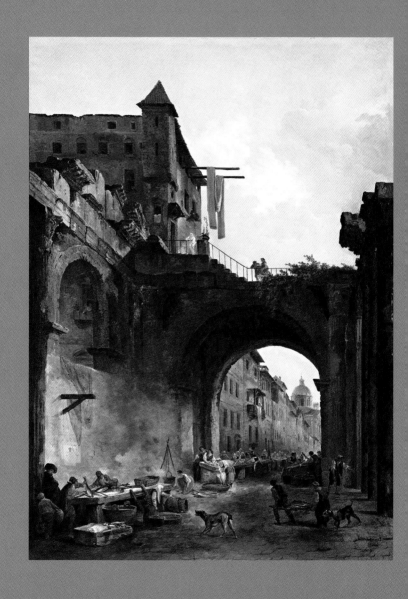

Oil on canvas, 63 × 45 inches (160 × 114.3 cm),
1784. Bequest of Henderson Green.

This remarkable and impressive example of the work of Hubert Robert, the eighteenth-century French painter of Italian views, was one of the first European masters to enter the Vassar collection, in 1880, less than one hundred years after it was painted. Its arrival was a result of luck and a drowsy art market. It was bequeathed to Vassar by Henderson Green, who stipulated in his will that he wished his executors "to sell my large oil painting providing they can realize therefore the sum of one thousand dollars. If they shall within one year from my decease, be unable to sell said painting … then in that event, I give and bequeath the said painting to Vassar Female College (23 July 1879)." In the Salon of 1785, Robert exhibited a painting of the Octavian Gate and fish market "5 pieds 6 pouces de haut," which was acquired by the Marquis de Montesquiou. The painting in question was sold in 1788. The Louvre owns a version of this subject that presumably is the work referred to in the literature. The Vassar painting is likely a second version produced by Robert owing to the popularity of the first. Robert's interest in the ancient sites in and around Rome was a product of his years of study in the workshop of Giovanni Paolo Panini. When he returned to France in 1765, he painted this subject matter often for an enthusiastic public. Robert later became an early curator of the Louvre under Louis XVI and keeper of the royal pictures. The Octavian Gate combines the grandeur of the imposing portal with its utility as a site for bustling quotidian commerce, evoking for the viewer the sights, sounds, and even smells of a city living comfortably with its history.

Nachi Pilgrimage Mandara

Ink, colors, and gold leaf on paper, mounted as a hanging scroll,
59 × 59 1/2 inches (149.9 × 151.1 cm),
Japanese, late sixteenth or early seventeenth century.
Purchase, Pratt Fund and Betsy Mudge Wilson, class of 1956,
Memorial Fund.

This anonymous painting depicts the sacred precincts of Nachi, a major site of syncretic Shinto and Buddhist worship in rural Japan on the island of Honshu. As part of the Nachi religious establishment's proselytizing and fundraising efforts, it was used by monks to narrate the countless factual and apocryphal tales associated with this sacred place. The painting is full of wonderfully expressive vignettes of the devotional activities that took place at Nachi over the centuries. The magnificent waterfall at Nachi, for example, which dominates the right of the painting, was considered the manifestation of a deity; in this painting, as is characteristic of the type, the renowned twelfth-century monk Mongaku is shown being rescued by two child-deities (Kongara Doji and Seitaka Doji) — so devoted was Mongaku to ascetic practice and worship under the sacred torrent, the legend goes, he almost perished. In the lower right of the painting, a small sailboat departs on a one-way trip to the mythical paradise Fudarakusen, its sail inscribed with an invocation of faith ("Hail to Amida Buddha"). This well-known practice involved worshippers of unshakable belief who willingly left behind the mundane world to seek the promise of the next, a practice that till the eighteenth century had many advocates. Among the recognizable sights and buildings of Nachi, numerous people of different social strata — warriors, aristocrats, monks, and commoners — engage in various activities. Altogether, approximately thirty Nachi pilgrimage paintings of this period are known, all but two in Japan, primarily in temples and shrines.

Nagasawa Rosetsu (Japanese 1754–1799)

A Terrapin with its Young

Brush and ink on paper, 46¹/₈ × 21¹/₂ inches (117.2 × 54.6 cm), ca. 1780.
Purchase Friends of the Frances Lehman Loeb Art Center.

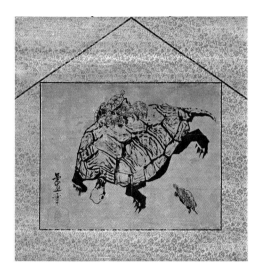

Rosetsu was a Maruyama painter. He was born and raised in the family of a low-ranking samurai of the Yodo clan in Yamashiro and was a student of the painter Okyo, but was dismissed from his studio for his unruly behavior. An intimate friend of the Confucian scholar Minagawa Kien, with whom he occasionally collaborated, Rosetsu was a highly eccentric individual and has been termed one of the small group of 'Individualist' painters of the Edo period. The sliding screens that he painted for a number of temples during his travels in the year 1787 mark his stylistic departure from the influence of Okyo. He also painted subjects of the Ukiyo-e (the 'Floating World'), particularly those of the 'beautiful women.' He was also fond of animal subjects, painting bold compositions with a touch of humor. This mother terrapin with its young is an example that suggests the engaging maternal bond between this unprepossessing animal and her offspring.

Joseph Wright of Derby (English 1734–1797)

Study of Rocks and Trees

Pencil and wash on paper, 14⁷/₈ × 21³/₈ inches (37.8 × 54.3 cm),
1774/75. Purchase, Suzette Morton Davidson Fund.

Although trained as a painter by Thomas Hudson in London, Joseph Wright
returned to his hometown of Derby in central England to live and work.
There, he was part of a group of scientists, intellectuals, inventors, and
artists known as the Lunar Society owing to their habit of meeting on
Monday evenings as close as possible to the time of the full moon. This
group included notables such as Josiah Wedgwood, James Watt, and Joseph
Priestly. Their scientific investigations inspired some of Wright's best-
known paintings. Wright made one journey to Italy, arriving in February
1774 and departing in June of the following year. While there he sketched
regularly, often in the company of his student Richard Hurleston. A portfolio
of these drawings was sold at auction in 1966, from which Vassar acquired
two large sheets, one of the entrance to a Roman ruin, and this delightful
and carefully observed study of light washing over rocks covered with what
seems to be leaves and lichen. Behind and to either side are small trees that
have rooted themselves in the rocks. This study, while grist for Wright's
painterly mill, is also a fine document of the wonder with which he, like
his fellow members of the Lunar Society, viewed the natural world, its rock
formation offering clues to the Earth's age and its manner of creation.

John Singleton Copley (American 1738–1815)
Portrait of a Man

Oil on canvas, 30 × 25 inches (76.2 × 63.5 cm), 1781.
Purchase, the Pratt Fund, the Friends of the Frances Lehman Loeb Art Center,
and the Francis Woolsey and Helen Silkman Bronson, class of 1924, Fund.

Copley is known as the first great American portrait painter, although he left
Boston in 1774 to live in Europe, settling in London for the remainder of
his life, where he was made a member of the Royal Academy. This bifurcated
career allows both America and Britain a legitimate claim to his artistic
legacy. This portrait of a man with the traditional appellation of "Colonel
Baker" is a work from the most productive and artistically accomplished
years of Copley's English period. It was painted three years after his great
Romantic *tour de force* of Watson and the Shark and in the same year as his
patriotic English history painting The Death of the Earl of Chatham. The honesty
and intelligence of the portrayal of this sitter rivals that of Copley's portrait
of his fellow expatriate American artist, Benjamin West (Cambridge, Massachusetts, Harvard University Art Museums) and was painted shortly after
that work was completed. It also has the livelier and less clinical brushwork
that denotes much of his work while in England. While many of Copley's
English portraits are essentially concerned with the trappings of privilege —
the rich fabrics, honorific decorations, and jewelry — this portrait of a yet
unknown sitter is the rare return by the master to portraits that penetrate
the psyches of the sitters. It assumes Copley's extensive first-hand know-
ledge of the man and his world.

George Romney (English 1734–1802)

The Honorable Mrs. Anne Seymour Damer

Oil on canvas, 30 × 25 inches (76.2 × 63.5 cm),
1779. Bequest of Sally Butzel Lewis, class of 1934.

This engaging portrait of the lovely Anne Seymour Damer dressed in rich pink satin is more than just another pretty face, as biographical research shows. She was the granddaughter of John, Duke of Argyll, and the god-daughter and cousin of Horace Walpole, who was charged with her care as a child and who encouraged her to study art. She was unhappily married and when her debt-ridden husband committed suicide in 1776 she embarked seriously on her artistic career, becoming an accomplished sculptor of an-imals. She also carved portrait busts of luminaries such as Admiral Horatio Nelson and executed a full-length standing image of King George III, now in the British Museum. This portrait of her was commissioned by her brother-in-law, the Duke of Richmond. She sat to Romney five times between 21 April and 9 June 1779. The portrait resided at Goodwood, the Duke of Richmond's estate, until 1932, when it was purchased by the father of its Vassar donor. Romney was not the only artist to capture Mrs. Damer's likeness, as she was also painted by Angelica Kauffmann, Richard Cosway, Joshua Reynolds, and Giuseppe Ceracchi.

Henry Fuseli (Johann Heinrich Füssli; Swiss 1747–1825)

The Dressing Room

Oil on canvas, 34³/₄ × 27⁵/₈ inches (88.3 × 70.3 cm), 1806/07.
Bequest of Suzette Morton Davidson, class of 1934.

The Swiss artist Johann Heinrich Füssli, like the American John Singleton Copley, left his native country to take advantage of the rich cultural life that resided in London in the late eighteenth century. He arrived in 1765 at the encouragement of the British ambassador to Berlin and pursued a career of writing and translating. He was eventually persuaded by Joshua Reynolds to study painting, a course of action that prompted an extended sojourn in Italy from 1770 to 1778. After his return, he spent his painterly career on subjects inspired by the study of the Antique and of great works of literature, particularly the works of Shakespeare and Milton. His paintings were charged with a highly Romantic emotionalism and his forms are often angular and facetted. His figural style concentrates on sculpturally muscled men derived from his study of Michelangelo, and on attenuated, Empire-waisted women rooted in the standard of beauty of his time. Images of women set in literary or secular contexts were prevalent in his art during the period 1790–1810, including a large number of brush and wash drawings of his wife in various poses and forms of fancy dress. Vassar's painting refers to lines 203–208 of William Cowper's lengthy (624-line) poem *The Progress of Error*. The specific characters in the painting are Folly, attended at the dressing mirror by servants, and Innocence, standing to one side by a piano and chastely dressed. Cowper sets the stage to their recognition thus:

> Folly and Innocence are so alike,
> The difference, though essential, fails to strike.
> Yet Folly ever has a vacant stare,
> A simpering countenance, and a trifling air;
> But Innocence, sedate, serene, erect,
> Delights us, by engaging our respect.

Cowper was one of the rare contemporary literary figures illustrated by Fuseli and the artist held him in the highest esteem.

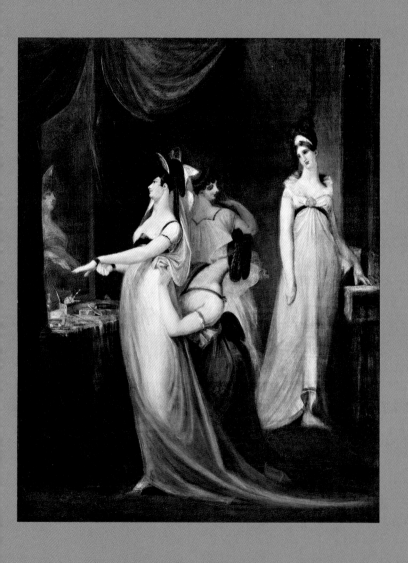

Thomas Rowlandson (English 1756–1827)

Scene in a Country Landscape

Watercolor, 4⅝ × 6 inches (11.7 × 15.2 cm), 1817.
Gift of Mr. and Mrs. Francis Fitz Randolph (Mary E. Hill, class of 1945–4).

An important artist during the golden age of English caricature from around 1780 to 1820, Thomas Rowlandson was esteemed for his humorous watercolors, drawings, and etchings gently skewering various social types. In many of these works, idealized landscapes and cityscapes serve as foils to scenes picturing the foibles and follies of a new city populace enjoying its leisure time. These harmonious backdrops aligned Rowlandson with the current trend in Georgian England of the romantic, picturesque landscape, the countryside being of prime importance for notions of rustic simplicity and beauty. Watercolor, prized for its accessibility and spontaneity, became central to the movement. This watercolor, Scene in a Country Landscape, fits well into the picturesque tradition, situating a peaceful couple within a graceful and charming rural landscape. It also fits well into the permanent collection of the Frances Lehman Loeb Art Center, complementing the over two thousand late eighteenth- and nineteenth-century British drawings and watercolors, mostly topographical and academic subjects, given to the college by Matthew Vassar in 1864 and purchased from the Reverend Elias Lyman Magoon at the time of the founding of the college. This particular sheet came from a gift of thirty-three watercolors and drawings by Rowlandson given in 1953 by Mr. and Mrs. Francis Fitz Randolph (Mary E. Hill, class of 1945–4).

Kezia Hawkes (English 1794–death unknown)
Sampler
Fabric, 12⁷/₈ × 12⁷/₈ inches (32.7 × 32.7 cm), 1803.
Gift of Mrs. James W. Packard (Elizabeth Gillmer, class of 1894).

This charming example of a needlepoint sampler is one of over three hundred European and American examples of this art form in the Frances Lehman Loeb Art Center's collection. It is the work of eight-year-old Kezia Hawkes and carries the inscription

> Virtue's the brightest Gem a Maid can wear
> Nor can the Indies boast one so fair
> All jewels far below its worth we find
> They but adorn the Body this the Mind.

In addition to the signature, date, and inscription, the young needlepoint artist has carefully laid out the alphabet in capitals, the first ten numbers, and, within a diamond-formed enclosure surrounded by intricate needlework, roses and other flowers. The symmetry and delicacy of her hand are remarkable. These works served as the foundation for a girl's education in the eighteenth and nineteenth centuries and are windows into its methodology. Their merits as instructional tools were debated by many of the intellectuals of the period, including Jean-Jacques Rousseau and Jane Austen.

John Ruskin (English 1819–1903)

The Church of the Annunciation at Vico Equense on
the Bay of Naples

Watercolor over charcoal on blue-gray paper,
15⁵/₈ × 11¹/₄ inches (39.7 × 28.6 cm), 1841.
Gift of Matthew Vassar.

John Ruskin was the most influential art critic and theorist of the nineteenth century who wrote in English. He was a great admirer and collector of the work of Joseph Mallard William Turner. He was also a compulsive draughtsman from an early age, but came to the realization that he could never achieve greatness by his art. His great powers of observation and keen analytical mind yielded drawings of great beauty and visual intensity. Ruskin was acquainted with the Reverend Elias Lyman Magoon, the guiding spirit behind the first Vassar art collection. Magoon acquired seven of Ruskin's drawings for the collection, including this one and a more controversial study made by the critic as a young boy. The identification of this view as the fourteenth-century church of the Annunciation at Vico Equense and its reconstructed sixteenth-century bell tower is a recent one. The village lies roughly three miles north of Sorrento and twenty-two miles south of Naples on the coast of the Bay of Naples. Ruskin journeyed there only once, in 1841. There are two entries in his diaries that refer to this location. The first on 26 February 1841:

A lovely drive yesterday from Castellamare to Sorrento. I could not see it well out of our close rattling carriage, but it was very perfect: all lovely rock promontory, orange and olive, and Vico placed *ad captandum* — thoroughly delicious.

And the second on 1 March:

Stopped at Vico to get a sketch, and failed, and bored myself.

It is altogether likely that his watercolor of Vico and its church was made on one of these occasions.

Asher B. Durand (1796–1886)

Through the Woods

Oil on canvas, 20¹/₄ × 15¹/₂ inches (51.4 × 39.4 cm),
1856. Gift of Matthew Vassar.

Asher Brown Durand started his artistic career apprenticed to an engraver in New York. With the encouragement of sponsors, he started to paint seriously in the 1830s. Travels to Europe in the company of other artists such as John Kensett and John Casilear opened his eyes to landscape painting as a serious pursuit, and he joined Thomas Cole as a spiritual co-leader of this field in America, ascending to the presidency of the National Academy of Design in 1845, a post he held until 1861. His early views on the method of painting directly from nature and observing its details closely were illustrated by an influential series of eight articles he published in 1855 entitled "Letters to a Landscape Painter." Through the Woods is a sun-dappled view of oak and beech trees in mid-summer crisscrossing near a stream, their limbs forming the natural equivalent of the tall and elegant vaulting system of a Gothic cathedral. The scene is near the banks of the Hudson River and one can recognize its location through the trees by the flat-topped landmass that descends rapidly to the river's edge. Elias Magoon knew Durand well and wrote to him about this painting after receiving it in 1856. With characteristically florid turns of phrase and flattery, Magoon summed up the essence of Durand's picture after studying what he called the artist's "Peep through the Woods" during his "Monday recreation":

As my eye rests on those great, calm children of the woods in the foreground, and then irresistibly falls back reach after reach through the glorious perspective to the still mightier hills in the remote distance, I have the fitting aisle of a majestic cathedral wherein to extemporize *te Deums* and High Masses at my own sweet will. Just now I was so uproarious in my devout admiration that Woodpecker blushed scarlet to the top of his head, and Squirrel snapped his ruffled tail and jerked up his left foot in rebuke.

Both woodpecker and squirrel can be found in the foreground of the painting.

Sanford Robinson Gifford (American 1823–1880)
The Roman Campagna
Oil on canvas, 6 × 10¹/₈ inches (15.2 × 25.7 cm), 1859.
Gift of Matthew Vassar.

Sanford Gifford was born and raised in upstate Hudson, New York. He briefly attended Brown University in Providence and moved to New York City in 1845. He studied and exhibited at the National Academy of Design. In spite of keeping his studio in New York, he managed to take extended annual sketching and painting trips to the scenic areas of the Hudson River Valley, the Catskill and Adirondack mountains, as well as to more distant locations such as the Maine and New Hampshire mountains. Yet, for all their dedication to capturing the 'sublime' attributes of the American landscape, Gifford and almost all the key artists of the Hudson River School traveled to Europe at least once and participated in the Grand Tour. Many American as well as

British and German artists gathered in loose colonies in Italy, particularly Florence and Rome. Sanford Gifford made two trips to Europe, the first from 1855–1857 and the second in 1868/69. From September 1856 to May 1857, Gifford was in Rome. This painting of the ruined aqueduct near the Appian Way outside of Rome was purchased by Elias Magoon, together with three other European oil sketches, in 1859, two years after Gifford's return to America. It is likely that this and the others were small replicas of larger paintings the artist made based on sketches done at the site. A larger, more finished version of this painting was exhibited at the National Academy of Design in New York in 1858.

Frederic Edwin Church (American 1826–1900)
Autumn in North America
Oil on board, 11¹/₄ × 17 inches (28.6 × 43.2 cm),
ca. 1856. Gift of Matthew Vassar.

This painting, like all works that bear the credit line to Matthew Vassar, arrived at the college at its founding in 1864. They were, for the most part, assembled by Elias Magoon, a Baptist minister, art collector, and early trustee of Vassar College. Magoon bought this work, along with two others, from the artist in 1856, still some eight years before his report to the trustees of Vassar College in 1864, convincing them of the need for a museum and collection of original works of art, rather than the copies that they were then acquiring. The work of Frederic Edwin Church is associated by most scholars with the apogee of the inventiveness and expressiveness of the Hudson River School, the work of several generations of artists who believed in exploring the range of natural beauty in the northeastern American landscape. Church himself created the largest, most sublime and operatic of these landscapes, usually not specific renderings of actual places but often Romantic amalgamations of the most striking and picturesque locales. Church's studio and home, Olana,

is located in Hudson, New York, some forty miles north of Vassar College. The large version of Autumn in North America resides there, originally stemming from a commission from Church's parents in that year. Vassar's painting, like most purchased by Magoon, is small in scale yet holds a tremendous amount of visual information, rendered with the same intensity of Church's larger works. The period of the 1850s was one of the most productive of the artist's career, culminating in several of his best known compositions, including possibly his two greatest *tours de force*, Niagara (1857, Corcoran Gallery of Art, Washington, D.C.) and Heart of the Andes (1859, Metropolitan Museum of Art, New York). This was also the time of his travels to South America in 1853, inspired by his reading of the journeys of German naturalist Alexander von Humboldt that served as a watershed of visual resources for much of his career, including that for Summer in South America, an oil sketch made in Ecuador, which is also in the collection at Vassar.

Jasper Cropsey (American 1823–1900)
Artist Sketching on Greenwood Lake
Oil on canvas, 20 × 33 inches (50.8 × 83.8 cm), 1869.
Gift of Georgia Potter Gosnell, class of 1951, and her daughter,
Elizabeth Gosnell Miller, class of 1984.

At 20 by 33 inches, this substantial painting, added to the collection in 2005, is larger than most of the American paintings in the original Magoon collection. Conveying the peace and tranquility of postbellum America removed from the intrusions of industry, it portrays a calm day on Greenwood Lake, a finger lake nine miles in length that straddles the New Jersey-New York border, not far from Cropsey's home in Warwick, New York, and a place that served the artist as a subject from 1843, when he was twenty years old. The tranquil water on which a single small sailboat glides, reflects the remaining greens, russets, and reds of the trees on the small island to the left, and even the pink and white clouds in the sky. In the foreground, the artist sits balanced on a log over the water's edge sketching while his dog wades in the shallow water. The entire composition is based on a gentle left-to-right movement that begins with the leaning *repoussoir* trees on the left, continues through the log on which the artist sits and its branches, which direct the eye into the open water and the boat, and ends with the gently rising hills on the opposite shore. Assured in composition and execution, the painting shows the artist at the height of his mature powers.

Charles Herbert Moore (American 1840–1930)

Morning Over New York

Oil on canvas, 12 × 30 inches (30.5 × 76.2 cm),
ca. 1859/60. Gift of Matthew Vassar.

This is one of four paintings purchased from the twenty-year-old Charles
Moore by Elias Magoon before the artist's style evolved into one more influenced by John Ruskin and the Pre-Raphaelites. Moore would later contribute
to the journal *The New Path*, the successor to *The Crayon* as the outlet for
Ruskinian criticism. This painting portrays a luminous sunrise over a
panoramic view of Lower Manhattan that ignites the pellucid atmosphere
with numerous subtle hues. Five years after painting this picture, Moore
moved his home and studio to Catskill, New York, after having narrowly
missed an appointment to Vassar as its first professor of art, for which he
was supported by letters from Frederic Church, Asher B. Durand, and Daniel
Huntington. University teaching seemed his destiny, however, for he became
a drawing instructor at Harvard in 1872, where he would go on to teach art
history courses as well, and was, eventually, made the first director of the
Fogg Museum, which opened its doors in 1895. During his early years at
Harvard, he was sent to Europe by Charles Eliot Norton to receive instruction
directly from Ruskin, although for all intents and purposes his career as an
independent artist was by that time behind him.

Charles Loring Elliott (American 1812–1868)

Portrait of Matthew Vassar

Oil on canvas, 96 × 63 inches (243.8 × 160 cm), 1861.
Gift of the Board of Trustees.

James Henry Wright (American 1813–1883)

Portrait of Matthew Vassar

Oil on canvas, 97 × 65³/₄ inches (246.4 × 167 cm), 1861.
Gift of the estate of Matthew Vassar.

The two full-length portraits of Matthew Vassar, the founder of Vassar Female College, cannot be studied independently because they provide complementary images of the man, the age in which he lived, and conventions in portraiture in general. Both paintings were executed in the same year, that of the founding of Vassar College and during the first year of its construction, as well as the first year of the American Civil War. The paintings are the same size and both were exhibited first in the autumn of 1861 in the Central Baptist Church in Poughkeepsie, where they were painted. They are, however, very different in appearance and intention. Elliott's painting is the quintessence of the 'official' state portrait, executed by the then reigning master of formal portraiture in America. Born in the small upstate New York hamlet of Scipio, Elliott received his artistic training in New York City in 1829, painting in the studio of the genre specialist John Quidor for six months. He returned to the Syracuse area, where he spent the next ten years painting portraits. His return to New York quickly established him as a talented portraitist at a time when this art form was at its height in America. There he exhibited almost annually at the National Academy of Design, submitting portraits of such distinguished sitters as William H. Seward, General J. C. Frémont, James Fenimore Cooper, and William Cullen Bryant, to name just a few. In 1861, the trustees of Vassar College commissioned Elliott to paint Matthew Vassar, for which he was paid the very generous sum of $1,200. He is shown in the 'Grand Style' presentation of the European masters, magisterially pointing from an impressive classical portico at a seemingly completed James Renwick-designed Main Building of Vassar College. In truth, the building was little more than a foundation at the time. The pose was captured, according to Benson Lossing, writing in July 1862, during an interview with Vassar when he was asked by Elliott if he thought his enterprise to build the college would succeed. "Succeed, Sir! I know it will

succeed — it *shall succeed*. What can prevent its success?" In this animated manner he answered Elliott's question and unconsciously assumed the position in which he stands in the picture. Mr. Elliott smiled, and said, "That is sufficient, Mr. Vassar. I have the design for the portrait, and the Expression I wished; we will now begin the picture." Vassar holds a gold-headed cane and has rested his top hat and gloves on the chair, which is partially hidden by the sumptuous red satin curtain. A copy of the Warwick Vase, a famous Roman antiquity, stands on the pedestal to his left.

The Wright portrait presents a very different Matthew Vassar, less Romantic, with fewer and homelier trappings. He is shown on the path above the gate-house of his 'country' residence, Springside, designed by the noted land-scape architect A. J. Downing, but, like Vassar College in 1861, yet un-finished. A reviewer for the *Poughkeepsie Telegraph* wrote in November, 1861, that Wright captured Vassar "as his friends know him and daily meet him," without the formal affectations of wealth and rank found in the Elliott portrait, and with his small dog, Tip, resting at his feet. This portrait was not an 'official' commission but a private one from Vassar himself, for which he paid Wright half the fee commanded by Elliott. While Elliott was known for using photography as a frequent source of reference for his portraits, in this case it is Wright's that seems much truer to the photographic likenesses of Vassar than is Elliott's more Romantic version.

James Ross and John Thomson
(Scottish ca. 1813–1895 and ca. 1808–1881)
A Happy Dream
Albumen print, 7 7/8 × 6 inches (20 × 15.2 cm), 1862/63.
Purchase, Horace W. Goldsmith Foundation Fund.

In the mid-nineteenth century, British art photographers imitated the work of academic painters through several methods: props, stock poses, painted backdrops, multiple exposures, and the manual reworking of both negative and print. All of these techniques are represented in this striking collaborative image. Early Edinburgh partners Ross and Thomson produced both daguerreotypes and calotypes (salted-paper prints from paper negatives), and were experimenting with albumen-based emulsions as early as 1849. James Ross operated a painting studio and might have painted the backdrop seen here, which, in a somewhat altered state, appears in genre-scene photographs sold under his name in 1863. This fine example of allegorical staging and combination printing was shown at the 1863 exposition of the London Photographic Society.

Peter Henry Emerson (American, born Cuba, active England 1856–1936)
Cutting the Gladdon
Plate 32 from Life and Landscape on the Norfolk Broads, 1886,
Platinum print, 7⁷/₁₆ × 9¹/₂ inches (18.9 × 24.1 cm), ca.1885.
Museum purchase, E. Powis and Anne Keating Jones, class of 1943, Fund.

Cutting the Gladdon is one of forty studies of rural labor that comprise Peter Henry Emerson's portfolio Life and Landscape on the Norfolk Broads (1886). The careful staging of Emerson's genre scenes of cane workers recalls the studio-based imagery of earlier Victorian camera artists, but Emerson's platinum prints differed crucially in their intended simulation of the qualities of human vision. In the name of what he called "naturalistic photography," Emerson focused his camera, like an eye, upon specific details within a larger scene, thus imparting a softening burr to all surrounding phenomena. By promoting the meaningful use of selective focus, and by accepting blurred gestures as the result of photographing people in action, Emerson signaled the beginnings of a modernist mode of photography that took authenticity for its chief concern. "Never shall we attain to the true secret of happiness," he wrote, "until we identify ourselves as part of nature." The credo is reflected in his subject matter and methods alike: Emerson's attention to East Anglia's rustic fen residents and his reliance upon scientific theories of optics signal his alert, if romanticized, conception of mankind's place in a larger scheme of nature.

Sir Lawrence Alma-Tadema (English, born the Netherlands 1836–1912)
An Exedra
Oil on panel, 15 × 23³/₄ inches (38.1 × 60.3 cm), 1869/70.
Gift of Mrs. Avery Coonley (Queene Ferry, class of 1896).

Much like the French academic painter Jean-Léon Gérôme, with whom he can
be compared, Sir Lawrence Alma-Tadema was a Victorian academic painter
who found a specialty that he could mine extensively during his career. While
Gérôme concentrated on the exotic and often romantic lure of the Middle
East, Alma-Tadema focused his attention on the presentation of scenes of the
classical past rooted in archeological precision and correctness. Alma-Tadema
was born in the Netherlands and received his early artistic training in
Antwerp, particularly from Baron Hendrik Leys. In the early 1860s he built a
commercial relationship with the influential art dealer Ernest Gambart, who
began to exhibit his work in London in 1865. At first there was critical resistance to his painting, but eventually success followed that induced the artist to
move his studio to Brussels. The year preceding the painting of An Exedra
found Alma-Tadema in Italy on an extended tour, and a cache of drawings
inspired by Pompeii survives from this trip. In May 1869, the artist's wife,
Pauline, died, and he did not paint for four months thereafter. He himself
suffered ill health later in the year and came to London for treatment. The
outbreak of the Franco-Prussian War, together with an infatuation with a
young Englishwomen, convinced Alma-Tadema to move his studio to London
in 1870, where it would remain for the rest of his life. Vassar's painting was
executed in December 1869, during this period of extreme transition in the
artist's life; it was begun in Brussels and finished in London. It portrays the
tomb of Princess Mamia, which lies outside the walls of Pompeii, formed as
an exedra, a semi-circular bench that affords a magnificent view of the Bay of
Naples. Exedrae were common gathering places for intellectual discussion.
The exedra motif would occur in a number of Alma-Tadema's paintings from
this period, and it is known that he owned a number of photographs of this
monument. In February 1892, he wrote to the art dealer Knoedler:

This is the round seat outside the gate of Herculaneum built on the ground upon
which the tomb stood of Mammia [sic], a great Pompian [sic] lady. The decree by
which the town of Pompeii granted this request to put up the seat stands in front
of it, engraved in marble. The tomb is seen behind … The slave of Holconius,
who carries his sunshade, sits on the pavement. Those seats on the wayside was
[sic] for the use of passersby to rest. The picture was finished and delivered to
Gambart on the 29th of December, 1869 …

Curiously, however, the painting bears the date 1870 in the artist's hand, so
perhaps a few adjustments were made early in the next year. It is tempting
to relate the portrayal of a tomb of "a great Pompian lady" to the death of his
wife, but the artist never indicated such an association.

Gustave Doré (French 1832–1883)

The Defense of Paris

Oil on canvas, 76 1/2 × 51 inches (194.3 × 129.5 cm), 1871.
Museum purchase, Suzette Morton Davidson, class of 1934, Fund.

Doré was a born illustrator, a prodigy who was making drawings to illustrate stories while still a young child. This interest led quickly to a career in art, beginning with drawings for Parisian journals made while still attending the Lycée Charlemagne. He then turned to painting (and sculpture), entering his first Salon in 1850. He made his reputation by illustrating many of the great works of world literature, including Dante's *Divine Comedy*, Milton's *Paradise Lost*, and the Bible. He was also a scathing social critic, publishing the illustrations to English journalist Blanchard Jerrold's *London: A Pilgrimage*, in 1872, an indictment of the gulf between the classes in contemporary England. Vassar's painting by Doré, The Defense of Paris, is one part of a trilogy of allegorical paintings entitled Souvenirs de 1870, a response in pigments to the humiliation France suffered at the hands of the Germans during the Franco-Prussian War. By skillfully managing a French ambassador's misstatement regarding Prussian attempts to dictate the next king of Spain, the German Chancellor Otto von Bismarck drew France into a war, declared by the Emperor Napoleon II on 15 July 1870. By 1 September the French army surrendered and the Emperor was captured. Paris was then besieged on 20 September and surrendered on 18 January of the following year. Doré himself was inside the capital at the time and wrote plaintively of the horrors of the invasions and the siege. Doré portrays a female allegory of the French Republic standing inside the gates of Paris surrounded by beaten French soldiers and distressed civilians. The entire painting is executed *en grisaille* except for the red and blue of the French flag that is held furled behind France's back. The entire mood is of disillusionment and defeat, yet the heroism of the Parisian populace is underscored. The remaining two paintings in the trilogy are somewhat more obscure in their allegorical references. One, entitled The Enigma, portrays a winged female figure (France) anxiously interrogating a Sphinx regarding, presumably, the outcome of the war, while Paris burns in the background. The second painting, The Black Eagle, shows the personification of the French Republic, her sword broken, protecting a fallen officer as a huge, menacing black eagle, a symbol of the German empire, swoops in for the kill.

Albert-Ernst Carrier-Belleuse (French 1824–1887)

Veiled Woman

Terracotta, 21 × 16³/₄ × 12 inches (53.3 × 42.5), after 1868.
Museum purchase, Louise Woodruff Johnston, class of 1922, Fund.

Carrier-Belleuse entered the École des Beaux-Arts in 1840, sponsored by the sculptor P.-J. David d'Angers. He became renown for his portraiture and was a prolific sculptor in many materials including marble, bronze, and alabaster, but his terracotta work is particularly distinctive. He also produced a series of fantasy busts often based on a single studio model. This bust, with its rendering in terracotta of a face swathed with diaphanous fabric sheer enough to allow the facial features to be recognized, is a *tour de force* of the artist's ability to overcome the limitations of a certain material (in this case clay) to suggest the illusion of something quite different. The air of mystery inherent in an anonymous, shrouded head and its traditional reference to funereal motifs holds the attention and stimulates the imagination of viewers. Carrier-Belleuse changed his signature from A. Carrier to A. Carrier-Belleuse in 1868. Since the Vassar bust carries the latter signature it must date from after this year, though its style suggests a date not much later than the early 1870s.

Jean-Léon Gérôme (French 1824–1904)
Camels at the Watering Place
Oil on canvas, 22¹/₂ × 32¹/₂ inches (57.1 × 82.6 cm),
1890. Gift of Mrs. Elon H. Hooker, class of 1894.

Gérôme was probably the most well known of the academic 'Orientalist' painters of the nineteenth century. His many portrayals of the exotic aspects of life in Ancient Greece and Rome, as well as more contemporary life in the Middle East and North Africa, stimulated the romantic and voyeuristic impulses of this audience and reflected the cultural fashions for things 'Eastern.' He became one of only three professors at the École des Beaux-Arts in 1864 and exercised great influence over a generation of academic painters. His vocal resistance to the painterly freedoms exercised by the Impressionists helped drive his art gradually out of style and, ultimately, into disfavor. He was, however, a prolific creator of images of exotic places and moments, and the consummate craftsman, ever seeking the perfection of the visual effect or surface of the thing being portrayed, particularly the female nude. Camels at the Watering Place was exhibited at the Salon of 1890 under the title L'Abreuvoir. It is typical of Gérôme's romanticized genre scenes of North Africa. While formulaic and, by this time, rooted in successful composition ensembles, the painting displays the artist's very sensitive rendering of the dappled lighting effects across the ground and ancient walls of the mosque.

Carl Frederik Aagaard (Danish 1833–1895)

Visitors on the North Shore of the Kullens Peninsula

Oil on canvas. 16¹/₂ × 23⁷/₈ inches (41.9 × 60.6 cm), 1880.

Museum Purchase, Friends of the Frances Lehman Loeb Art Center Fund.

The career of Carl Frederik Aagaard is a footnote to the history of nine-teenth-century painting, yet this small landscape capturing the intense effects of evening light during the long summer days in Sweden is a brilliant example of the largely neglected field of Danish landscape painting. Aagaard studied at the Danish Academy of Art in Copenhagen and later became the student of Peter Christian Skovgaard. He traveled twice to Italy in the 1870s, became a member of the Danish Academy in 1874 and was made professor in 1892. He is known for his fluidly painted landscapes of the coastal areas of Denmark and Sweden. In the Vassar painting, two ladies with parasols and a boy in a vest and cap relax among the rocks near the north shore of the Kullens Peninsula, the western-most point in Scania (Skåne), Sweden. It overlooks the maritime confluence of the Danish Straits (Öresund) and the Kattegat, and is still today largely a nature preserve for tourists and hikers. The strong raking light of what is presumably early evening ignites the surfaces of the rocky coast.

Edvard Munch (Norwegian 1863–1944)
The Seine at St. Cloud
Oil on canvas, 24 × 19⅝ inches (61 × 49.8 cm), 1890.
Gift of Mrs. Morris Hadley (Katherine Blodgett, class of 1920).

This cityscape by Munch, one of a half dozen that he painted during a so-journ at St. Cloud from the end of December 1889 to the beginning of May 1890, at first strikes the viewer as uncharacteristic of the artist, having none of the intensely vibrating forms or extreme melancholic subject matter of the artist's later work. Upon closer inspection, though, it is easy to discern the less-than-tranquil ambience where strong shadows cast by the moonlight project a slightly sinister quality, and the lights shimmering on the water serve as a precursor for the more extraterrestrial lighting effects of Munch's later, more disturbing, work. The branches of the tree along the footpath droop in a manner suggestive of the sadness associated with such trees as willows. When the painting was given to Vassar in 1962, it was one of only a very few oils by the artist in American museums. Arthur Hadley, the son of the donor, was an early proponent of Munch's art and his mother purchased the painting for him sight unseen. His reaction was disappointment and Mrs. Hadley was anxious to re-sell the painting but could find no buyers. She then suggested to the chairman of the Vassar art department that the painting be given to the institution and the gift was accepted, but without great enthusiasm since the painting was not representative of Munch's art and looked more "like a Whistler." Vassar immediately explored the possibil-ity of selling the painting, but fortunately did not pursue the issue thanks to the rise in the artist's reputation and the advocacy of scholars in the field.

Alfred Ronner (Belgian 1851–1901)
The Botanist
Oil on canvas, 23⁵/₈ × 19¹/₈ inches (60 × 48.6 cm), ca. 1875.
Gift of Rezin A. Wright.

This charming genre scene was a very early acquisition by Vassar College, entering the collection in 1880. The painter is the little known Alfred Ronner, son and student of his better known mother, Henriette Ronner-Knip, a popular painter of cats and dogs. He was, however, a gifted painter and illustrator in his own right, although he also sold his mother's paintings and published editions of prints. This painting was commissioned by an Antwerp patron of the artist. It portrays a subject close to the hearts of the Victorian public, an earnest young woman improving her mind by applying herself to scientific study. Surrounded by books and dried botanical specimens, and probably in a state not unlike that of many Vassar students of the day, she seems to convey the inner tranquility that results from enlightenment owing to study.

William Trost Richards (American 1833–1905)

Legendary England: Tintagel

Watercolor on paper, 9³/₄ × 15³/₄ inches (24.8 × 40 cm), 1882.

Gift of Elias Lyman Magoon.

In 1882, the American Pre-Raphaelite painter William Trost Richards ex-ecuted a series of watercolors of specific English locations representative of different themes. These sites were painted regularly by the artist during his residence in London from 1878 to 1880. Elias Magoon gave Vassar seven of the subjects depicting Mythical, Legendary, Monastic, Scholastic, Romantic, Commercial, and Regal England, the year after they were painted. Magoon was a dedicated collector of Richards's work and also donated over forty of his watercolors to the Metropolitan Museum of Art in New York City. For Legendary England, the artist chose Tintagel Castle on the wind-swept Cornish coast in Devon, thought to have been King Arthur's castle, a myth revived in Alfred Lord Tennyson's popular *Idylls of the King*, published in 1859. The site was a much-visited one by artists and writers, including J. M. W. Turner. The ruins of the early thirteenth-century castle built by Richard, Earl of Cornwall, half-brother of Henry III, are portrayed by Richards as a daunting citadel extending organically from the dramatic rising rocky cliff.

Charles Courtney Curran (American 1861–1942)
Shadow Decoration
Oil on canvas, 18 × 32 inches (45.7 × 81.3 cm),
1887. Museum purchase.

This beguiling painting, arguably the most popular among visitors to the Frances Lehman Loeb Art Center, was purchased by Vassar's first professor of art and gallery director, Henry Van Ingen, for $300 from the autumn 1887 exhibition at the National Academy of Design in New York City. It is one of four laundry paintings by Curran that were executed in that year. While it was painted the year before Curran went to Europe, it ably demonstrates his knowledge of certain predicates of Impressionism, particularly the play of light and the design influence of Japanese woodcuts, while retaining elements of the genre tradition in American painting, particularly the quiet, strong, and noble portrayals of working women of Winslow Homer.

Here, we see a laundress, anonymous yet visibly strong, absorbed in her task. The bed sheets on the line create a scrim through which the viewer encounters a play of violet and gray shadows created by the limbs of what might be a peach tree. Their silhouettes, however, conjure in our minds Asian bamboo. Furthermore, the manner in which the clothesline arbitrarily cuts across the upper margin of the painting on a slight diagonal is itself a convention of Japanese woodcuts. As a result, Shadow Decoration is a fascinating hybrid creation combining stylized artistic conventions from abroad with an honesty and simplicity rightly associated with the still youthful American Republic.

Paul Gauguin (French 1848–1903)

Pots en grès. Chaplet

Gouache and graphite, 12 × 15 3/4 inches (30.5 × 40 cm), ca. 1888.
Bequest of Sarah Hamlin Stern, class of 1938, in memory of her husband,
Henry Root Stern, Jr.

Gauguin, one of the most influential of French Post-Impressionist artists, explored a variety of artistic media in addition to drawing and painting. These included woodcuts, carved wooden sculpture, and ceramics. Through the printmaker Félix Bracquemond, Gauguin was introduced in 1886 to the ceramicist Ernest Chaplet, whose stoneware technique (grès), previously understood in France only in a utilitarian sense, was considered artistically highly evolved. Gauguin was taught how to work in this material and over the next ten years produced around one hundred objects, including the two vases that appear in this drawing — the Leda Vase (represented twice) and the Portrait Vase in Unglazed Stoneware of a Woman Wearing a Snake-Belt. Both vases survive and are in private collections. This medium allowed Gauguin to make works of seeming utilitarian art, thus emphasizing and incarnating the cross-cultural references that most interested him.

Henry Ossawa Tanner (American 1859–1937)

A View of Palestine

Oil on canvas, 22 × 37 inches (55.9 × 94 cm), ca. 1898/99. Gift of Mrs. Walter Driscoll (Margaret L. Weyerhaeuser, class of 1923), Mrs. F. Rodman Titcomb (Elizabeth L. Weyerhaeuser, class of 1915) and Mrs. Robert J. Sivertsen (Sarah Weyerhaeuser, class of 1930).

Henry Tanner was born in Pittsburgh of mixed European, African, and Native American ancestry. He studied at the Pennsylvania Academy of Art with the renowned Realist Thomas Eakins. Finding no success in his attempts to practice art in his own country, he became an expatriate and was well received in Paris, where he made his home beginning in the early 1890s. He became known for his depictions of religious subjects and spent the remainder of his life as an expatriate, painting in a loose and evocative style largely influenced by contemporary French art. In 1898, he made a trip to the Holy Land in conjunction with a visit there by the German Emperor William II and Empress Augusta Victoria. While there he visited Palestine and painted the Vassar canvas. His impressions were summarized in a reminiscence that Palestine was a place of "great barren hills that can blossom like a rose ... a natural setting of great tragedy." Vassar's painting, stemming from this period rich in personal exploration, is illustrative of his richest period, when he interpreted the world he saw in an immediate manner and style still fresh with first impressions.

Marsden Hartley (American 1887–1943)

Indian Composition

Oil on canvas, 47 3/16 × 47 inches (119.9 × 119.4 cm), 1914.
Gift of Paul Rosenfeld.

Born in Maine, Marsden Hartley was a key member of the group of American Modernists promoted by Alfred Stieglitz before the Second World War at his various galleries in New York. Hartley spent the years 1912–1915 abroad in Paris and, later, Berlin, returning only briefly in 1914 to install an exhibition of his work at Stieglitz's 291 Gallery. Indian Composition, painted in the spring and summer of 1914, was one of seven paintings from a series entitled *Amerika* that he executed in 1914/15. The general theme explored his internal conflicts as an American enamored with life in Germany on the eve of war. The first paintings in the series utilize the symbols of Native American life, and the later ones add motifs taken from German folk traditions. The Vassar painting has been viewed as reflecting Hartley's respect for the Native American's life, lived in harmony with the land, as well as the fascination with this culture viewed through the eyes of Germans, whose familiarity with the American Indian was influenced largely by popular adventure novels such as those by Karl May. The meaning of this painting can best be understood through the words of the artist himself, who in November 1914 wrote to Alfred Stieglitz that "I find myself wanting to be an Indian — to paint my face with the symbols of that race I adore, to go to the West and face the sun forever — that would seem the true expression of human dignity." Indian Composition was owned by the music critic and writer Paul Rosenfeld before it was given to Vassar following his death by his executor, Edna Bryner Schwab. It was Rosenfeld who in Hartley's obituary characterized him as "the gaunt eagle from the hills of Maine."

Clarence Kerr Chatterton (American 1880–1973)

Clinton Square, Newburgh

Oil on canvas 27¹/₂ × 35¹/₄ inches (69.8 × 89.5 cm),
1917. Bequest of Leila Cook Barber.

Since Vassar College opened in 1865, there has been a total of only four professors of painting during a continuous history of one hundred and forty
years. C. K. Chatterton was the second in this impressive succession, serving
from 1915 to 1948. He was born in Newburgh, New York, on the west bank of
the Hudson River, and studied at the New York School of Art, founded by
William Merritt Chase. It was a school for illustrators and his teachers were
Howard Chandler Christy, Walter Appleton Clark, and, later, Robert Henri.
It was there that he forged lasting friendships with Rockwell Kent, Gifford
Beal, and, most importantly, Edward Hopper, with whom he made regular
trips to sketch and paint the Maine coast. Two years after being hired by
Vassar College, Chatterton painted Clinton Square, Newburgh as seen from
his office in the Highland Bank building that he rented for the summer of
1917. This painting, imbued with the bustling impressions of life in a thriv-
ing downtown, extends the principles of Henri's teaching of Realism and
observations of daily life. The painting is also suffused in the light and
atmosphere of a summer's day, where strong shadows are cast by the solid
structures that line the street. Chatterton would go on to exhibit at the
Wildenstein, Macbeth, and Chappellier galleries, and live to see his work
collected by such institutions as the Metropolitan and Brooklyn museums.

Georgia O'Keeffe (American 1887–1986)
East River No. 3, Grey Blue with Snow
Oil on canvas, 12 × 32 inches (30.5 × 81.3 cm), 1926.
Bequest of Mrs. Arthur Schwab (Edna Bryner, class of 1907).

Georgia O'Keeffe painted a series of over a dozen views of the East River from the rooms she shared with her husband, Alfred Stieglitz, on the thirteenth, and subsequently other floors, of the Shelton Hotel from 1925 until 1936. They depart greatly from her more familiar images of flowers and trees and, instead, present the geometry of an urban environment in various moods. They are also more representational than the works of the preceding decade, largely in response to the extreme Freudian interpretation to which her work had been subjected. The painting was first exhibited at Stieglitz's Intimate Gallery located in room 303 of the Anderson Gallery building in 1927 as part of an exhibition of forty recent paintings by the artist. This gallery was the successor to his defunct 291 Gallery and a precursor to An American Place. It was there that Edna Bryner Schwab likely purchased the work. Mrs. Schwab was a devoted client of Stieglitz's and it was her role as executrix of the Paul Rosenfeld estate, and her own bequest, that brought to Vassar its superb collection of the American Modernists launched by Stieglitz's efforts.

Georgia O'Keeffe (American 1887–1986)

Spring

Oil on canvas, 35¹/₂ × 30¹/₈ inches (90.2 × 76.5 cm), ca. 1922.
Bequest of Mrs. Arthur Schwab (Edna Bryner, class of 1907).

Georgia O'Keeffe began exhibiting with Alfred Stieglitz in 1916 at his famous 291 Gallery. After it closed its doors (with an O'Keeffe show) in 1917, the artist exhibited at the Anderson Gallery, where in 1923 a solo exhibition of one hundred paintings was held entitled *Alfred Stieglitz Presents One Hundred Pictures: Oils, Water-colors, Pastels, Drawings, by Georgia O'Keeffe, American.* Spring was included in this exhibition. The paintings by O'Keeffe from the period 1918–1924, which are among her most evocative studies of nature, were inspired by her travels to Texas, the Southwest, and Maine. Most are, like Spring, presented with the forms directly against the picture plane, the absence of a foreground creating an intimate confrontation with the viewer. The resulting sense of magnification is strengthened by O'Keeffe's use of vibrant colors.

Georgia O'Keeffe (American 1887–1986)

Two Figs

Oil on board, 7 3/4 × 5 3/4 inches (19.7 × 14.6 cm), 1923.
Bequest of Mrs. Arthur Schwab (Edna Bryner, class of 1907).

Part of the rich holdings of Stieglitz-circle material, this painting by O'Keeffe is a fine example of her ability to lend to an everyday object, plant, or flower a sense of monumentality. The placement of the two very differently shaped figs against the folds of the stark, bright, white background invest them with an ambiguous identity. As with so many of O'Keeffe's natural forms, they suggest other, parallel objects. Their scale has no specific comparative reference, thus a small painting such as this one can seem in reproduction to suggest something much larger. This painting was included in the early O'Keeffe retrospective exhibition at the Museum of Modern Art in New York held in 1946. Like a number of the other works of the Stieglitz group in Vassar's collection, it was purchased by the donor directly from Stieglitz's gallery, An American Place.

Charles Demuth (American 1883–1935)
Apple and Acorn Squash
Watercolor on paper, 12³/₄ × 17³/₄ inches, ca. 1929.
Gift of Angeline James Pool, class of 1940,
in memory of Oliver B. James Fane.

Charles Demuth, along with Georgia O'Keeffe, Arthur Dove, John Marin, and
Marsden Hartley, was one of the group of modernist artists championed by
the impresario photographer and gallery owner Alfred Stieglitz. Demuth's
art ranged widely from the colorful pastimes and distractions of urban envir-
onments to lovingly depicted simple beauties of the rural American scene
around Lancaster, Pennsylvania. Such a watercolor as this study of fruit
and vegetables is part of a body of superb work by the artist in this very
demanding medium, of which Demuth was one of its greatest twentieth-
century practitioners. The Vassar watercolor is tentatively dated, based on
what seems to have been a second watercolor in a private collection of the
same squash and bowl that is signed and dated 1929. The influence of
Cézanne is unmistakable in Demuth's still-lifes, but they have an interest
in faceted forms and geometry that also draw on Cubist prototypes.

Arthur Dove (American 1880–1946)
Broome County from the Black Diamond
Oil on canvas, 18¹/₄ × 24 inches (46.4 × 61 cm), 1931/32.
Bequest of Mrs. Arthur Schwab (Edna Bryner, class of 1907).

A native of central New York State, Arthur Dove went to New York City to earn a living as an illustrator in a fairly traditional style. Travels to Europe in the first decade of the twentieth century exposed him to incipient movements of modern art and shortly after his return to New York in 1909 he met Alfred Stieglitz, whose influence would in many ways change his life. He exhibited for the first time at Stieglitz's 291 Gallery the next year and regularly there and at Stieglitz's other galleries for the next three decades. From the 1920s onward, his work was avidly collected by Duncan Phillips in Washington, D.C. The Phillips Collection today owns more of Dove's work than any other museum. Vassar graduate Edna Bryner Schwab was also a frequent client of Stieglitz's and bought two paintings by Dove as well as a number of others by Stieglitz-circle artists. Broome County from the Black Diamond was purchased by Schwab from Stieglitz's An American Place in 1932. It is one of Dove's small vibrant landscapes from a period when his pure abstractions begin to integrate elements of direct observation and naturalistic rendering. His life and work at this time benefited from a greater level of personal and financial security, and also a move back to his former residence in Geneva, New York. There he paid closer attention to billowing natural forms and their occasional metaphorical references.

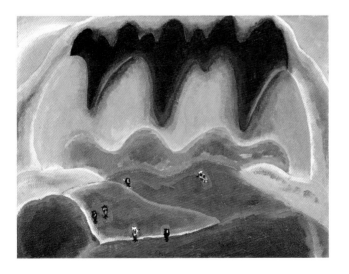

Florine Stettheimer (American 1871–1944)

Natatorium Undine

Oil and encaustic on canvas, 55¹/₂ × 60 inches (141 × 152.4 cm), 1927.
Gift of Ettie Stettheimer.

Although born in Rochester, New York, Florine Stettheimer was trained in an academic manner at the Art Students League in New York City. Her mature style, however, was laden with naïve images of personal iconography and fantasy. Hers was a private world of art making, and her affluent circumstances allowed her the luxury of not having to sell her paintings. She had her first and last gallery exhibition at Knoedler's in 1916. She and her sister, Ettie, lived together at the center of a stimulating cultural set that included friends such as Marcel Duchamp, Virgil Thompson, Cecil Beaton, Elie Nadelman, Alfred Stieglitz, Carl Van Vechten, and critic Henry McBride among others. Vassar donors such as Kirk Askew, the art dealer, and Paul Rosenfeld, the art and music critic, and Vassar faculty such as Agnes Rindge were also part of this social milieu; a fact that ensured an exhibition of the artist's work at Vassar in 1949, the year *Natatorium Undine* was given to the college. The painting receives its title from the water nymph 'Ondine' from the fairy tale by Friedrich de la Motte Fouqué. It turns up in the poetry of T. S. Eliot and as a character in Edith Warton's novels. The swimming pool or 'natatorium' is the gathering place for carefree relaxation. Seated at the table in the upper left is Fania Marinoff, the wife of Carl Van Vechten. Next to her is the artist, often an observer in her own paintings, reclining on a chaise decorated with roses. Her sister Ettie sits on the left, at the side of the pool, wearing a horizontally striped bathing costume. The rest of the figures suggest both the canon of feminine beauty and the activities of the Jazz Age —music, dance, and sybaritic pursuits.

Pablo Picasso (Spanish 1881–1973)
Glass, Guitar and Musical Score
Oil and sand on canvas, 21¹/₄ × 32 inches (54 × 81.3 cm), winter 1922/23.
Gift of Virginia Herrick Deknatel, class of 1929 in honor
of Frances Daly Fergusson, President of Vassar College, 1986–2006.

There are over thirty works of art by Picasso in the Vassar art collection spanning nearly every decade of the artist's career from a Barcelona-period drawing of 1899–1900 to a late etching of 1968. Glass, Guitar and Musical Score is the Art Center's fourth and earliest Picasso painting. It is the only Picasso still-life in the collection and reflects his late 'Baroque' Cubism following the First World War, when the compositions were dramatically flattened and painted in pastel tones. The rounded, raw sienna form at the center of the composition, representing the body of a guitar, glitters faintly with fine-grained sand, a subtle textural accent that offsets a background of creamy pale yellow and periwinkle. The harmonious, decorative schema and musical theme are reminders that by 1922 Picasso had been immersed for half a decade in the high-society world of dance and theater, both through his marriage (1918) to dancer Olga Koklova and through several commissioned stage, costume, and curtain designs for Serge Diaghilev's *Ballets Russes* and other companies. Vassar acquired its first Picasso, a 1927 linocut, in 1941.

Pablo Picasso (Spanish 1881–1973)

Shepherd and Goat (Pastorale)

Tempera and ink on paper mounted on canvas,
27 × 34 inches (68.6 × 86.4 cm), 22 July 1946.
Bequest from the collection of Katherine Sanford Deutsch, class of 1940.

After the Second World War ended, Picasso moved to Antibes in the south of
France. There his subject matter began to incorporate aspects of mythology
as he became more interested in the cultural traditions of the Mediterranean
region. Thus, a work such as this one summons the serenity and simplicity
of the pastoral existence that seemed to serve as something of an antidote
for the strife that captured the artist's attention for the preceding decade.

Pablo Picasso (Spanish 1881–1973)

Head of a Woman

Oil on canvas, 24 × 18 inches (61 × 45.7 cm), 1953/54.
Gift from the collection of Mr. and Mrs. Alexander E. Racolin.

According to an inscription in charcoal on the back of this canvas, Picasso worked on the painting from 24 March 1953 until 23 May 1954. It was at this time that Picasso became interested in a young woman named Sylvette David, who worked at a ceramic studio near Picasso in Vallauris, and painted her a number of times. Over the years, the Vassar painting has been exhibited under the title Tête de Sylvette and Tête de Femme. While the woman's ponytail is somewhat suggestive of Sylvette's Brigette Bardot-like mane, her features, even in Picasso's most painterly presentations, were finer. Hence, it is more likely that this head is of a more generic sort, painted at a time when Picasso's position vis-à-vis the women of his life (the departure of Françoise Gilot and the arrival of Jacqueline Rocque) was in a state of significant transition for the seventy-two-year-old artist.

Robert Delaunay (French 1885–1941)

Rhythme

Oil on artist's board, 29¹/₂ × 20⁷/₈ framed (74.9 × 53 cm),
ca. 1932–1937. Bequest of Gladys K. Delmas, class of 1935.

Robert Delaunay worked during the first half of the twentieth century as a color theorist in the tradition of his nineteenth-century precursors Michel-Eugène Chevreul and Paul Seurat. His colorful, fractured images of the Eiffel Tower, and his first color disc paintings of the years prior to the outbreak of the First World War, became France's answer to the Futurist and Vorticist movements in Italy and Britain. Delaunay worked in Paris until 1914, and again after 1920. It was there, according to his wife Sonia's journals, he made the acquaintance of Jean Delmas, a publisher of artists' books at the studio of the artist Emmanuel Gondouin in 1935. Delmas married a Vassar graduate, Gladys Kriebel, in 1937, and husband and wife patronized a number of French artists for the next several decades. Delaunay and the Delmases met on at least two more documented occasions in the 1930s. The Delmas collection contains two additional Delaunay prints (one inscribed "à Delmas, à toute amitie") in addition to many works by the artists in the same circle in Paris in the 1930s, including Gondouin, Matisse, Fougeron, Pignon, and Gischia. This painting by Delaunay is unique in having been painted within a frame that, itself, was decorated by the artist to enhance the composition.

Henri Matisse (French 1869–1954)

Jazz

Portfolio of stenciled prints, each 16⅝ × 25¾ inches (42.2 × 65.4 cm), 1947.
Gift of Mrs. John D. Rockefeller 3rd (Blanchette Hooker, class of 1931).

These twenty *pochoir* prints by Matisse are perhaps the freest expression of his late career. The paper cut-outs were worked on by Matisse at his home in Vence between 1943–1946 while he was often in ill-health and frequently confined to bed or his wheelchair. They were then printed as stencils in an edition of one hundred by the publisher Tériade for his Editions Verve in 1947. These were done without text while the one-hundred-and-fifty-page book by the same name with Matisse's text, written in his own script, was published in a larger edition of two hundred and fifty copies. The text and images were not related, hence the ability of the illustrations to stand on their own merits. The images were largely inspired by Matisse's memories of the circus, popular legends, music halls, and his travels. In this series, images of acrobats co-habit with those of Icarus or the wolf from *Little Red Riding Hood*. The artist likened the act of cutting pure colors with scissors to that of the sculptor carving into stone. The intense and vibrant images are a summation of his love of color and movement.

Margaret Bourke-White (American 1904–1971)
Self-Portrait

Gelatin silver print, 12¹/₂ × 9¹/₄ inches (31.7 × 23.5 cm), ca. 1933.
Museum purchase, Horace W. Goldsmith Foundation Fund.

Self-taught and unapologetically ambitious, photojournalist Margaret Bourke-White handled her public image as adeptly as she did a camera. In 1929, with the start of her prominent role at the nascent *Fortune* magazine, Bourke-White recorded the construction of the Chrysler Building. Falling in love with both the stylish tower and the publicity value it promised, she opened her studio and office there. Here she poses on a sofa in the anteroom of her high-rise quarters, leafing through a portfolio of photographs made on her three voyages (1930–1932) to Soviet Russia. Bourke-White's characteristic air of dashing self-assurance is offset — to a comical degree that may help to explain her smile — by the lace frills on her dress, a feminine (and quite uncharacteristic) touch. That the portrait's setting helps to convey the sitter's up-to-the-minute spirit is no accident. Bourke-White had assigned the design and outfitting of her office to her friend John Vassos (1898–1985), an illustrator and industrial designer who enjoyed an unusual command of machine-age elegance. Vassar's print, in fact, once belonged to Vassos, who owned other Bourke-White photographs illustrating his product designs, including a close-up of the Art Deco clock seen here. This exquisitely made and preserved print provides a perfect case of chicken-and-egg aesthetics: what was, for Vassos, a gratifying document of his design acumen, was for the photographer an ideal image of herself at the top of her game.

Alexander Calder (American 1898–1976)

The Circle

Sheet aluminum, ceramic, wood, string,
35⁷/₈ × 31³/₈ × 31³/₈ inches (91.1 × 79.7 × 79.7 cm), 1934.
Gift of Agnes Rindge.

In 1931, Alexander Calder introduced a new sculptural art form — the mobile — and thus embarked on what would prove to be the most fertile decade of his career. This followed on the heels of a life-altering visit he paid to the Paris studio of Piet Mondrian in 1930, at which time he began to understand the nature of abstraction and his desire to work in this manner. Prior to this time his work had consisted largely of bent wire 'drawings' in a simple yet representative mode. The Circle is part of a small group of early mobiles on fixed bases that Calder produced in the mid-1930s. In January 1935 Calder wrote to 'Chick' Austin, director of the Wadsworth Athenaeum in Hartford, offering him The Circle, which was then housed in the studio of Calder's father, for an upcoming exhibition. In this letter he gave very detailed instructions on its installation. The sculpture was exhibited at Vassar in the spring of 1936 and bought by Vassar art professor Agnes Rindge at that time.

Arshile Gorky (Vasdanig Manoog Adoian;
American, born Turkish Armenia 1904–1948)
The Horns of the Landscape
Oil on canvas, 30 × 34 inches (76.2 × 86.4 cm), 1944.
Gift from the collection of Katherine Sanford Deutsch, class of 1940.

In 1920, Vasdanig Manoog Adoian arrived in the United States from his
native Armenia. After making his living teaching art in Watertown, Massachusetts, and Providence, Rhode Island, he moved to New York in 1925 and
changed his name to Arshile Gorky, as an homage to the Russian author.
His early work was largely influenced by Picasso and, in the 1930s, he
received several important public arts commissions. In the 1940s his work
grew increasingly influenced by the European Surrealists such as Miró
and Matta, and during this time his paintings became more animated and
turbulent. The Horns of the Landscape represents a very mature example of this
Surrealist work. It is somewhat unusual within the context of Gorky's total
output by virtue of the areas where the colors seems to bleed and run down
the canvas, suggesting that the work is delicate and virtually dematerializing
before your eyes. Gorky experimented with this technique with only a few
paintings during the years 1944/45, one key example of which is presently in
the collection of the Albright Knox Museum in Buffalo.

Mark Rothko (Marcus Rothkowitz;
American, born Latvia 1903–1970)
No. 1 (No. 18, 1948)
Oil on canvas, 67¹¹/₁₆ × 55⁷/₈ inches (171.9 × 141.9 cm),
1948/49. Gift of Mrs. John D. Rockefeller 3rd
(Blanchette Hooker, class of 1931).

Born Marcus Rothkowitz, Rothko came to the United States with his family in 1913, receiving his education at Yale University for two years before going to New York to become a professional artist. Through the period 1947/48, Rothko worked in a largely figurative style that then began to transmogrify into what becomes his classic phase around 1950, soft colored rectangles superimposed on another field of color, simultaneously suggesting a tranquility and tension among these areas of color. Within this development, the Vassar painting plays a very important role, being one of just a handful of works that fully articulate the transition from the realm of the somewhat recognizable to that of the completely abstract. In No. 1 (No. 18, 1948), Rothko painted a group of various round, square, triangular, and bulbous forms that are applied to a reddish-orange ground over which a more sienna colored soft rectangle floats like a cloud. Thus, the work becomes absolutely pivotal as one can look at this painting and simultaneously understand his origins and his future as a painter. Half of Rothko's total output of painted work date after 1948, making the Vassar painting literally a midway point in - numbers and style. He would have another twenty-two years to paint the remainder of his oeuvre before he took his own life on 25 February 1970. The Rothko painting is one of the most requested paintings for traveling exhibitions from the Vassar collection.

Jackson Pollock (American 1912–1956)
Number 10, 1950
Oil, enamel, and aluminum paint on canvas laid down on fiber board,
65 × 36¹/₂ inches (165.1 × 92.7 cm), 1950.
Gift from the collection of Katherine Sanford Deutsch, class of 1940.

The year 1950 was that of greatest productivity for Jackson Pollock, during which he created over fifty paintings. It was also the year that he was extensively photographed at work by Hans Namuth, giving us the images of the artist we conjure now when looking at his finished paintings. Namuth visited the studio on 1 July 1950 and captured the artist working on two large canvasses, One: Number 31, 1950 and Autumn Rhythm: Number 30, 1950. The Vassar painting is entitled Number 10, 1950 which logically suggests it was started early in the year, though Pollock's working method was not that regimented. Number 10, 1950 is unusual in two respects within Pollock's oeuvre. First, it is in a vertical format and, as such, exceptional. Second, it is a painting executed on a reddish-brown canvas rather than the more frequent white gesso, a support that Pollock would occasionally turn to at this time. 1950 was also the year when he executed a number of square paintings directly on brown masonite, supplied by his brother, that created a background quite similar to the look of the Vassar canvas, which itself is backed by a similar fiber board. Recent scholarship has suggested that this painting and a number of other works by Pollock were influenced by Native American fertility imagery, particularly that of the Hopi in Arizona.

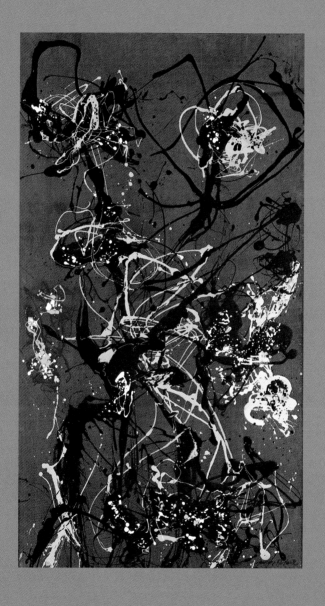

Balthus (Balthasar Klossowski; French 1908–2001)
Le semaine des quatre jeudis
Oil on canvas, 38¹/₂ × 33 inches (97.8 × 83.8 cm), 1949.
Gift from the collection of Katherine Sanford Deutsch, class of 1940.

The title of this painting translated literally is "The week of four Thursdays."
It refers to the French tradition of early dismissal of students from their
classes on Thursdays, thus a week filled with Thursdays conjures an image
of languor during this fantasy vacation from school. Balthus, descended
from Polish nobility, was best known for his enigmatic images of pubescent
girls lost in various forms of self-absorbed reverie. The Vassar painting is
typical of this aspect of his art, though the eroticism of the subject is a bit
underplayed. The presence of the cat was often used by the artist as a foil
for the innocent and artless sensuality of the young girls. In this case, its expression suggests a greater malevolence. A number of preliminary drawings
and paintings for this major composition survive in collections in Europe,
America, and Australia. Le semaine des quatre jeudis was purchased by Vassar
alumna Katherine Sanford Deutsch directly from the Pierre Matisse Gallery
in 1952 as she was in the process of assembling a small collection of European and American contemporary paintings to install in her recently con-
structed home in Greenwich, Connecticut. Vassar's strong holdings of post-
war modern art is due largely to her generosity.

Willem de Kooning (American, born the Netherlands 1904–1997)
Untitled (Three Women)
Oil and crayon on paper, 20 × 26³/₈ inches (50.8 × 67 cm), ca. 1948.
Gift of Mrs. Richard Deutsch (Katherine W. Sanford, class of 1940).

One of the key members of the group of Abstract Expressionists who were active in New York, the Dutchman Willem de Kooning worked steadily throughout the 1940s on studies that would evolve into his series of monumental paintings of women during the 1950s. Evoking the sensuous courtesans of Picasso's Les Demoiselles d'Avignon of 1907, de Kooning creates a tumble of interlocking forms, some clearly legible as body parts, others less so. The figures with their mask-like faces are set off from a background of strongly contrasting shades of yellow, red, orange, purple, green and blue, creating a primitive and aggressive planar assembly of figures in movement. This de Kooning and two others were the first gifts by Mrs. Deutsch to the Vassar collection and were bought directly from the artist at his studio when she visited him in the company of Thomas Hess, critic and author of early books and articles on de Kooning.

Joan Miró (Spanish 1893–1983)
Painting (Birds, Personages, and Blue Star)
Oil and casein on canvas, 51^1/$_2$ × 38^3/$_4$ inches (130.8 × 98.4 cm), 1950.
Gift from the collection of Katherine Sanford Deutsch,
class of 1940.

Painted in Barcelona and dated 17 March 1950, this excellent example of Miró's mature period of Surrealist and biomorphic forms is one of what is known as his 'slow' paintings from 1949/50, more planned compositions than his complementary 'spontaneous' paintings from the same years. Like several other works collected by Katherine Sanford Deutsch, this painting was sold to the collector by Pierre Matisse. The work is painted on raw, unprimed canvas and forms a capricious assemblage of lighthearted Surrealist hieroglyphs in an antic display. Its naïveté and dependence on the primitivism of pre-historic cave paintings such as those in Altamira, Spain, link Miró in a spiritual and familiar manner with the indigenous traditions of Iberia. Miró was once quoted as stating that all art degenerated after that of the cave dwellers. Some critics are uncomfortable with too much emphasis on these attributes of Miró's art, and stress that he was also affected by both the political unrest of Spain and Europe in the mid-twentieth century as well as by the overheated intellectual environment he encountered during his residence in Paris at the time of the Spanish Civil War. Some would see the occasional nightmare in the dream images. Nonetheless, his attitude regarding the childlike and naïve aspects of painting ran parallel to that of another artist well represented in the collection of the Frances Lehman Loeb Art Center — Alexander Calder, whose art is also rich in primary colors and elegant yet somewhat random seeming forms.

Karel Appel (Dutch 1921)

Child and Beast II

Oil on canvas, 39¹/₈ × 59¹/₈ inches (99.4 × 150.2 cm), 1951.
Gift of Mrs. John D. Rockefeller 3rd (Blanchette Hooker, class of 1931).

Appel was a founding member of the CoBrA group of avant-garde painters who took their name from the first letters of the three cities central to their development, Copenhagen, Brussels, and Amsterdam. Their leaders were Asger Jorn, Pierre Alechinsky, Corneille, Appel, Constant, and Carl Henning Pederson. The Danish influence is thought to be the most acute in their development, though their composition and view as a loosely cemented movement was distinctly Pan-European. They came together in a post-war European environment that emphasized a lack of finesse in painting with a surging primitive component that is easily grasped in this mature work by

Appel. Also contributing to their aesthetic was the study of children's drawings and the influence of folk traditions. This painting was included in
the Museum of Modern Art's influential 1955 exhibition, *The New Decade*,
which featured the work of twenty-two European painters and sculptor, and
which traveled across the United States and acquainted an American public
with the work of such newcomers as Appel, Francis Bacon, Jean Dubuffet,
and Pierre Soulages. Appel's first American gallery exhibition took place the
previous year at the Martha Jackson Gallery, likely the original source for this
painting.

Henry Moore (English 1898–1986)
Double Standing Figure
Bronze, H. 87 inches (221 cm), 1950.
Gift of Edgar Kauffman, Jr.

This large bronze by one of the twentieth century's leading sculptors holds an important position in Henry Moore's career. It presents two casts of a single figure of a distinctive combination of biomorphic and geometrical components (what Moore himself called "skeletonic"), one figure turned at approximately 90 degrees from the other. The single Standing Figure was exhibited at an important outdoor installation of Calder's work at Battersea and was positioned before a lake. Moore relates that when it returned from the exhibition, a second cast had already arrived in his studio: "… having them both at the studio I was able to try out a double figure arrangement. For some little time before working on this figure, I was thinking of making four separate figures standing in a row on the same base … But one never finds the time to carry out all one's plans, and when the two casts of this single figure were together I saw a chance to carry out at least part of the first unrealized conception." Moore continues, "doubling up of the two figures increased the complexity of the formal relations and intensified the kind of rhythm that the single one had. The two figures can't help having a certain unity since they are in fact the same figure, but in placing them together I made sure that each figure presented a different view from the other whichever way one looked at them." Only two casts were made of the Double Standing Figure. The donor of the work, Edgar Kauffman, Jr., was the son of the Pittsburgh department store magnet of the same name, who commissioned Frank Lloyd Wright to design the family's country house, Fallingwater.

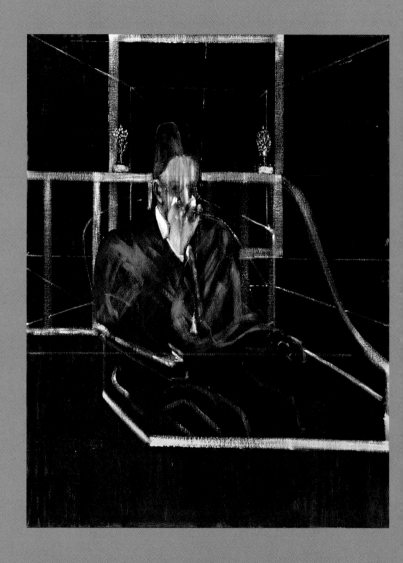

Francis Bacon (English 1909–1992)
Study for Portrait IV
Oil on canvas, 60 × 45³/₄ inches (152.4 × 116.2 cm), 1953.
Gift of Mrs. John D. Rockefeller 3rd
(Blanchette Hooker, class of 1931).

The paintings of Francis Bacon deal almost exclusively with the human figure, often subject to a tortured or grotesque transformation. This particular work is one of a series of eight paintings executed in 1953, most of which were exhibited together shortly thereafter at the Durlacher Brothers Gallery in New York, Bacon's first exhibition outside England. The Vassar painting was purchased directly from the exhibition by Blanchette Hooker Rockefeller and given to the college less than two years later during her tenure as a college trustee. They are based — as are a number of other works from the 1950s — on Diego Velásquez's Portrait of Pope Innocent X of 1650. Bacon admitted to being "haunted and obsessed by the image ... by its perfection." Nonetheless, in spite of making many trips to Rome, he never ventured to the Doria Pamphili Gallery to see the object of his obsession. At the end of his life, he claimed that he hated these paintings and regretted very much painting them because the Velásquez was perfect already and there was, after all, really nothing he could do further.

Ben Nicholson (English 1894–1982)

Graffito

Oil and pencil on masonite, 60 × 36 inches (152.4 × 91.4 cm), 1955.
Purchase, Mrs. John D. Rockefeller 3rd (Blanchette Hooker, class of 1931) Fund.

Ben Nicholson came from a family of English artists. Both his father and mother were successful painters. His career followed a fairly predictable path for a young artist in the twentieth century — some formal training followed by extensive travel and, finally, a return to England, where he participated in exhibitions in London from the early 1920s onward. He gained an international reputation following the Second World War featuring many individual and group shows in Paris, Athens, Prague, Brussels, Hamburg and Amsterdam, to name a few cities. His art was championed in the United States by Durlacher Brothers, whose director, Kirk Askew, was the step-father of Pamela Askew, a Vassar graduate herself and an important member of the art faculty beginning in the 1950s. A number of European artists otherwise little known at the time in the United States made their way into Vassar's collection via this route. Around 1950, Nicholson began a series of major still-life paintings that attempted to integrate Synthetic Cubism with the pure abstraction of Mondrian. It was also a time when the artist was reaching the height of his creative powers. Graffito comes at the very end of this group of paintings but, unlike the others, it is painted on brown masonite that is allowed to show through and becomes an active composition element. The surface is strongly textured and looks ahead to the next phase of abstract reliefs produced after 1955. While Nicholson was well known for his lack of interest in a painting's title, stating that titles were "literature, not art ... merely a tag," his choice of a title in this case does lend itself to more a more specific reference to the surface of the painting.

Hans Hofmann (American, born Germany 1880–1966)
Au Printemps
Oil on canvas, 48 × 36 inches (121.9 × 91.4 cm), 1955.
Gift from the collection of Katherine Sanford Deutsch,
class of 1940.

Although the United States claims Hans Hofmann as its own, this distinction is not based solely on the amount of his life that he spent here but on his tremendous impact as a teacher during the advent of the Abstract Expressionist movement in America. Born in a small Bavarian village, he moved with his family to Munich at the age of six. He received his early art training there, and with financial backing from a patron moved to Paris when he was twenty-four. There he became familiar with the leading lights of contemporary art including Picasso, Matisse, and Robert Delaunay, who arguably had the greatest influence on the young artist. By the time the First World War broke out he was back in Germany, where he opened his first school of art in 1915. After the end of the war, the school became a magnet for an international clientele, including American artists such as Louise Nevelson and Alfred Jensen. His American contacts led to invitations to teach in Berkeley, California, as early as 1930, and he decided to leave Germany permanently in 1933, establishing a school in New York City with a successful summer program in Provincetown, Massachusetts. Two years before his first major retrospective at the Whitney Museum in New York, Hofmann painted Au Printemps, a paean to joy found in the natural world. Lighter in touch and palette than many of his large paintings, it uses the white of the primed canvas to suggest a meadow where wildflowers lightly grace its surface and shimmer in the crisp light of a spring day.

Isamu Noguchi (American 1904–1988)
Bell Image (Polygenisis)
Cast iron, H. 31¹/₂ inches (80 cm), 1956/57.
Gift of Mr. and Mrs. Frederic Ossorio.

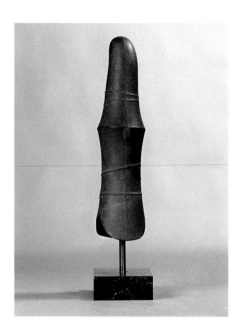

Noguchi was born in Los Angeles of a Japanese father and American mother
but grew up in Japan from the age of two. He returned to America in 1918
for his higher education. After a brief period of medical studies at Columbia,
Noguchi decided to become a sculptor, a career to which he devoted himself
full-time in 1924. Bell Image (Polygenisis) was created when Noguchi began to
spend more of his time in Japan after 1950 and is inspired by his exposure
to the *dotaku* bells, which are used for rituals and serve also as emblems
of wealth and power. It also draws on the forms of early Haniwa idols of
Japan's prehistory. This sculpture was created at a time when Noguchi was
working on a number of large commissions, including the gardens for the
UNESCO headquarters in Paris and the 2500 birthday of the Buddha in
New Delhi, but was executed, together with a number of other cast iron
works by the artist, in Japan.

Nancy Graves (American 1940–1995)
Five Fans Lampshades and Lotus
Bronze with polychromed patina, H. 81 inches (205.7 cm), 1982.
Bequeathed by the artist.

Nancy Graves, a member of the class of 1961, is Vassar's most well-known artist alumna. She pursued graduate study at Yale University and became an accomplished sculptor, painter, printmaker, and video artist. Her sculpture stems primarily from nature and her own interest in the natural sciences, and frequently bear exotic titles such as Catepelouse, Fayum, or Archaeoloci. Often the sculptures from the 1980s are assemblages of various cast objects including seed pods, palm fronds, and other vegetal forms. The Vassar work carries a more prosaic and descriptive title, isolating the primary elements — the lampshade base, the large lotus leaf from which emerges the crown of five Japanese fans, connected by slices of what appears to be a gourd or root. The manner in which the elements are connected suggests a slow torsion that encourages the viewer to address it from multiple points of view. This work is quite typical of the delicately balanced layers of unrelated objects that, together, appear to have metamorphosed into a new and bizarre species of plant.

Nancy Graves, by © Nancy Graves Foundation/Licensed by VAGA, New York, NY

Naoya Hatakeyama (Japanese 1958–)
River 2

From the series River,
Chromogenic print mounted on aluminum,
21 1/4 × 10 1/2 inches (54 × 26.7 cm), 1993/94.
Museum purchase, Horace W. Goldsmith Foundation Fund.

In 1993, the year Naoya Hatakeyama made the first exposure in what was to become his River series, photography's imminent reinvention by digital technology was only beginning to be glimpsed. The photographs of the series, which portray the cement-lined Sumida River as it winds throughout Tokyo, are produced entirely by means of predigital photographic processes, but the questions they pose about the medium's veracity point the way ahead to a changed medium. For each of the photographs, Hatakeyama stood at the Sumida's longitudinal center, pointed his camera downriver, and positioned his lens at the exact height where the cement walls to the left and right bank outward. The sideways banquet camera he used produced vertical images of a perfect 2:1 vertical format, which the receding horizon line splits into two perfect squares, one atop the other. Above the horizon one sees the physical city; below it, a 'floating world' of rippling reflections. Taken as a whole, the series pushes to the forefront many accidental aspects of photography, calling into question its claims as an impartial, fact-recording system of representation. The luscious but unreal colors of River 2 result from a lengthy exposure made under artificial lighting. The print's outer edge — an inevitable feature of a photograph, but seldom of more than marginal concern to the viewer — here might be said to constitute the subject matter of the picture, at the center of which one finds only a black void. Finally, the bold horizontal line that splits the picture in two emphasizes photography's structural basis in single-point perspective — a pictorial convention inherited from the art of drawing. 'Straight' though its means of creation may be, River 2 declares itself, in equal parts, a product of attention and artifice.

Vik Muniz (Brazilian, active USA 1961–)
Beggar I, after Rembrandt

From the series Pictures of Wire,
Gelatin silver print, 34³/₄ × 28¹/₈ inches (87.3 × 71.4 cm), 2001.
Museum purchase, Advisory Council for Photography.

Vik Muniz, by © Vik Muniz/Licensed by VAGA, New York, NY

Vik Muniz creates ephemeral *trompe l'oeil* constructions out of unlikely materials and directs them at a highly defined audience: the eye of his camera. For his Pictures of Wire series, the trained sculptor arranged tiny scraps of metal, including pins, needles, paper clips, and staples, on a horizontal white surface. The result, as seen here: line-for-line imitations of Rembrandt's beggar etchings of the 1630s (a series represented in the Art Center's Felix M. Warburg Collection). After photographing his handiwork, Muniz swept this assemblage aside and started the next. Muniz seeks to create what he cheerfully calls the "worst possible illusion": a representation which, when examined closely, falls far short of resembling its model, yet which induces a casual eye to 'see' the intended image without raising the slightest suspicion. His work, entertaining as it is, prompts important insights about illusion, perception, and our propensity to 'recognize' — that is, to *know-again* — the images through which we know the world.

Jenny Holzer (American 1950–)
For Elizabeth, Twenty Granite Benches
Each 60 × 18 × 24 inches (152.4 × 45.7 × 61 cm), 2006.
Museum purchase, Friends of the Frances Lehman Loeb Art Center
in honor of Frances Daly Fergusson.

This very recent site-specific sculptural commission executed by the concep-
tual artist Jenny Holzer consists of twenty dark-green granite benches, each
of which is inscribed on its seat with both published and unpublished verses
by the Pulitzer Prize-winning poet Elizabeth Bishop, a member of Vassar's
class of 1934. The work was commissioned in honor of Frances Fergusson,
President of Vassar College (1986–2006) on the occasion of her retirement.
The benches are arranged on alternating sides of a 775-foot landscaped path
that runs from the central dining facility for the campus, designed McKim,
Meade, and White, to the original Main Building, designed by James Renwick. Drawing upon Bishop's strong images of love, growth, beauty, and
struggle, the benches serve as a metaphor for the complexities of the journey
every undergraduate makes while inhabiting, as well as enriching, the Vassar
landscape. As one slowly absorbs the poetry while traversing the path, one
takes part in a concomitant physical, aesthetic, and intellectual journey.
Holzer has worked in this stone medium since the 1980s, often inscribing
them with aphorisms or truisms of her own authorship, often of strong
social or political significance. She has also delivered these messages in the
form of xenon projections and light emitting diode (LED) displays.

Information

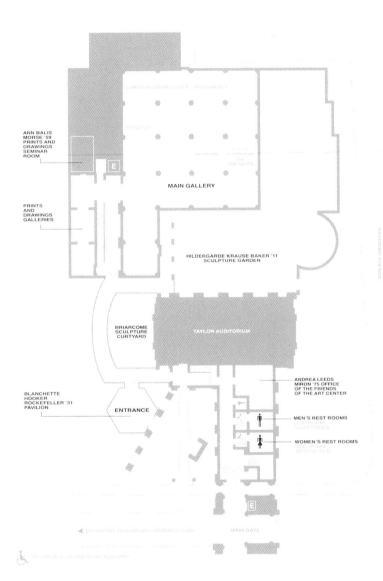

ANN BALIS
MORSE '59
PRINTS AND
DRAWINGS
SEMINAR
ROOM

PRINTS
AND
DRAWINGS
GALLERIES

MAIN GALLERY

HILDERGARDE KRAUSE BAKER '11
SCULPTURE GARDEN

BRIARCOME
SCULPTURE
CURTYARD

TAYLOR AUDITORIUM

BLANCHETTE
HOOKER
ROCKEFELLER '31
PAVILION

ENTRANCE

ANDREA LEEDS
MIRON '75 OFFICE
OF THE FRIENDS
OF THE ART CENTER

MEN'S REST ROOMS

WOMEN'S REST ROOMS

Address	The Frances Lehman Loeb Art Center
	124 Raymond Avenue, Box 703
	Poughkeepsie, New York 12604–0703
	For information and directions:
Website	fllac.vassar.edu
Phone	845.437.5237
Hours	Tuesday to Saturday: 10:00–5:00
	Thursday: 10:00–9:00
	Sunday: 1:00–5:00
	Closed: Mondays
	The Art Center is closed Easter, Thanksgiving Day,
	and from Christmas to New Year's Day.
	Admission is FREE
	Group visits are welcome.
	All galleries are wheelchair accessible.
Membership	Support for the art center is provided by the Friends of the
	Frances Lehman Loeb Art Center. For more information and
	details on membership and benefits, call 845.437.5243
Groups and School Visits	There are numerous activities and tours which we can offer.
	For educators, guided tours and tour group information, contact
	the Coordinator of Public Education and Programs,
	on 845.437.7745
Exhibitions Schedule	For a recorded schedule of events,
	call 845.437.5632
Regulations	No food or drink is permitted in the galleries. Parcels,
	briefcases, backpacks, and umbrellas are not permitted in the
	galleries. Only those objects owned by the Frances Lehman
	Loeb Art Center may be photographed. Tripods are not allowed.
	All photographers should check in with security guards
	on staff.
Coatrooms Rest Rooms Lockers	Coatrooms are located to the right of the entrance pavilion.
	Storage lockers are located in the atrium just before entering
	the galleries. Rest Rooms are next to the coatrooms. All bookbags,
	backpacks, packages and umbrellas must be deposited in the
	coatrooms or lockers before entering the galleries.

Artists' Rights

© for the works by the artists, their heirs, or assigns, with the exception of Karel Appel, by © 2007 Karel Appel Foundation/Artists Rights Society (ARS), New York; Francis Bacon, by © 2007 The Estate of Francis Bacon/ARS, New York/DACS, London; Balthus, by © 2007 Artists Rights Society (ARS), New York/ADAGP, Paris; Margaret Bourke-White, by © Estate of Margaret Bourke-White; Alexander Calder, by © 2007 Estate of Alexander Calder/Artists Rights Society (ARS), New York; Arshile Gorky, by © 2007 Artists Rights Society (ARS), New York; Naoya Hatakeyama, by © Naoya Hatakeyama; Hans Hofmann, by © 2007 Estate of Hans Hofmann/Artists Rights Society (ARS), New York; Jenny Holzer, by © 2007 Jenny Holzer, member Artists Rights Society (ARS), New York; Georgia O'Keeffe, by © 2007 Georgia O'Keeffe Museum/Artists Rights Society (ARS), New York; Willem de Kooning, by © 2007 The Willem de Kooning Foundation/Artists Rights Society (ARS), New York; Henri Matisse, by © 2007 Succession H. Matisse, Paris/Artists Rights Society (ARS), New York; Joan Miró, by © 2007 Successio Miró/Artists Rights Society (ARS), New York/ADAGP, Paris; Henry Moore, by © Reproduced by permission of the Henry Moore Foundation; Edvard Munch, by © 2007 The Munch Museum/The Munch-Ellingsen Group/Artists Rights Society (ARS), New York; Ben Nicholson, by © 2007 Artists Rights Society (ARS), New York/DACS, London; Isamu Noguchi, by © 2007 The Isamu Noguchi Foundation and Garden Museum, New York/Artists Rights Society (ARS), New York; Pablo Picasso, by © 2007 Estate of Pablo Picasso/Artists Rights Society (ARS), New York; Jackson Pollock, by © The Pollock-Krasner Foundation/Artists Rights Society (ARS), New York; Mark Rothko, by © 2007 Kate Rothko Prizel & Christopher Rothko/Artists Rights Society (ARS), New York.